"Marion,
Give Us a Smile!"

"Marion, Give Us a Smile!"
An American Immigration Story
...and a Detective Story

The extraordinary story of how, in 1922, New York politicians saved a poor Jewish butcher and his family after Ellis Island officials ordered them deported on arrival.

LISA ZORNBERG

"Marion, Give Us a Smile!"

Copyright © 2019 Lisa Zornberg

Disclaimer

This book is a memoir. It reflects the author's recollections of experiences, family stories, and historical research. While the persons mentioned in this book are real, some individual characteristics may have been changed, some events have been compressed, and some dialogue has been recreated.

Cover image: New York: M. Froomkin, circa 1927. Original photograph of Marion Scher. Owned by the author.

ISBN: 978-0-578-49521-7

Printed in the United States of America

This is for my children, Aden and Ethan,
to whom I gift the rich inheritance of how our family
came to America, and all else I hold dear.

Contents

Introduction 1

How My Grandmother Went to Harvard Law School 1

But Wait! The Making of a History Detective 6

Chapter One: Life in the Old World 9

Stories Are Worth More than Diamonds 9

My Brother's Stink .10

My Beginnings 11

Husiatyn 12

Sarah and Meyer 13

The Cat's in the Cradle 15

My Earliest Memory: Praying for Mama in the Cemetery . .16

Eating Raw Onions to Stay Alive 17

Cousin Elka Becomes a Widow 19

"Now You Live in Poland" 19

The Oldest Girl 20

Jake, Our Angel 21

Enter: The History Detective 21

What's in a Name? .21

Marion's Birthdate .23

Marion's Birthplace: A Brief History of Husiatyn 24

Kopyczynce 33

Chapter Two: Journey to America 37

From Poland to France .37

Oh, What a Sight!—The SS *Berengaria* 38

Boarding the *Berengaria* 39

Looking Forward 40

That's Not a Black Cherry! 40

In for the Shock of Our Lives at Ellis Island: Disaster! 42

Enter: The History Detective 44

Putting on Historical Lenses 44

The Open Spigot—That Is, before It Closed 44

A Brief (and Riveting!) History of Jews in America
    Leading Up to 1922 .46

Jacob and Louis Green: Making It in the New York City
    Garment Industry 53

The Closing Spigot 57

The American Eugenics Movement—
    The Backlash to the Spigot 58

And Then Americans *Really* Freaked Out:
    The Red Scare of 1919 and 1920 63

"Whose Country Is This" Anyway? 64

The Spigot Gets Tighter—the 1921 Emergency
    Quota Law 66

The Scheers' Unheralded Angel on Their
    Journey to America: HIAS 72

Time for Show and Tell: The Scheers' Entries in the
    Ship Manifest 75

How Meyer Scheer Answered the Questions, as
Recorded in the Ship Manifest 77

Physical Stuff 77

Race, Occupation, Destination 78

Money 78

The SS *Berengaria* Docks in New York Harbor 79

My Theory as to How Meyer's Heart Murmur
Came to Be Detected at Ellis Island 80

**Chapter Three: Thirty-Three Days and Nights at
Ellis Island**. 83

We Were Pulling Our Hair Out. 83

Aunt Annie, Our Savior. 84

Enter: The History Detective 85

Taking on the Legend. 85

How Politicians Saved the Scheers 87

September 22, 1922: Put in Detention 87

September 23, 1922: The Scheers Fight Exclusion 88

September 26, 1922: Testimony at Ellis Island 89

Meyer's Testimony .91

Uncle Jake's Testimony 92

Aunt Annie's Testimony. 94

Joseph Scheer's Testimony. 95

September 27, 1922: HIAS at Work 98

October 1, 1922: Yom Kippur on Ellis Island. 98

October 4, 1922: The Case Goes to Washington 99

October 7, 1922: Politicians Go on Record—
Congressmen Albert Rossdale and
Nathan Perlman and Power Broker Simon Wolf 99

October 9, 1922: Efforts by the Greens 104

October 10, 1922: The Scheers' Case Is Reconsidered . . . 105

October 12, 1922: A Gut-Wrenching Proposal 106

October 14, 1922: Enter an Even Bigger Gun—
Senator William Musgrave Calder 108

October 16, 1922: Yet Another Political Gun Enters—
This Time, Congressman Christopher D. Sullivan, a
Democrat 111

October 19, 1922: The Momentous Train Ride to
Washington, DC 114

October 20, 1922: The Gates Open 115

October 24, 1922: "Duly Admitted" at Last 116

October 25, 1922: Wrapping Up the Niceties 117

Tackling the *Why* 117

Theory One: It's a Horse, Not a Zebra 118

Theory Two: There's a Zebra Somewhere in This Barn . . . 122

What Happened to the Politicians
Who Saved the Scheers? 124

Foray into Fiction: Two Proposed Hollywood
Movie Plots about the Secret *Why* 131

Movie Plot One: The Love Story 131

Movie Plot Two: The Organized Crime Story 133

Chapter Four: Coming of Age in America 137

The Cat's Pajamas 137

The Gifts of a Plucked Chicken 138

Brooklyn Bound 139

Blossoming 140

Meeting Emanuel 141

So Now You Know 144

Enter: The History Detective (for the Last Time) 145

Return to Ellis Island 145

Becoming Americans 147

The Deepening of Roots amid Tumultuous Times 148

Harvard Bound 152

Afterword 159

Personal Reminiscences about My Grandmother 159

Acknowledgments 165

Sources and Notes 169

Chapter One 169

Chapter Two 170

Chapter Three 174

Chapter Four 178

Afterword 178

"No kind of life is worth leading if it is always an easy life. . . . I have never in my life envied a human being who led an easy life. I have envied a great many people who led difficult lives and led them well."

—Theodore Roosevelt

Introduction

How My Grandmother Went to Harvard Law School

IT WAS 7:30 A.M. ON A Monday, and there we were: Ten brand new, nervous, first-year law students—1Ls we were called—assembled around a large table, having breakfast with the dean. I looked around Dean Robert C. Clark's spacious, private office and soaked it in. So well appointed, a mixture of wood, glass, and exotic objects (mounted tribal masks and such). I imagined a world and life of deep intellectual pursuit.

It was the fall of 1991. What were we students doing there, break-fasting with the dean in his private office? Well, that previous June, Harvard Law School had been ranked last in some quality-of-life survey of American law schools. Unacceptable! In response, Harvard decided to turn up the charm for its new arrivals. That September, the school rolled out a welcome mat for its arriving 1Ls, dividing us into O-groups (orientation groups). Each group was to be mentored by a different faculty member. Dean Clark, the head of Harvard Law

1

School, in a show of support for the program, decided to mentor one O-group personally—mine.

So there we were, at the start of the semester for our kick-off mentorship meeting. The dean looked pleasant but was utterly silent. He was a shy and lovely man, I would come to learn. We waited intently for him to begin speaking. One minute passed. Three minutes. Five. Awkward silence while we politely sipped coffee and stabbed at the Danish.

At last, an attempt was made. "So," the dean sputtered, "how did your friends and families react when they heard you were going to Harvard Law School?"

The question registered enthusiastically with my classmates. The guy across the table exclaimed in a Southern drawl: "My hometown was so impressed I'm going to Harvard, they wrote an article about me in the local paper! I walked around all summer like a celebrity."

Another: "You should have seen my boss's face when I dropped the *H-bomb* on him." Supportive smiles and head nods.

Round the table the students went, praising the Harvard name. The dean looked relieved not to have to say another word.

It rubbed me the wrong way. Chalk it up to being drilled with anti-elitist attitudes by my parents, two New York City public schoolteachers. "Actually," I said, when the discussion got around the table to me, "my grandmother had never heard of Harvard until last week." The dean nearly spit out his coffee.

"My grandmother lives in Brooklyn," I continued. "She's not originally from this country. When I spoke to her on the phone last week, she said, 'Lisa, I was sitting on the boardwalk with Ethel and Pearl, and they said this place you're going to is something special. You've been hiding it from me. What's it called?'"

"Harvard, Grandma. What are you talking about? I haven't been hiding it from you—I went to college here too—"

"But you didn't tell me it's a special place."

"It is. It's an excellent school, Grandma."

"So what are you learning there? Arithmetic?"

"Well, right now I'm studying to be a lawyer."

"Ah, such a *kup* [head] on you. Lisa, darling, there will be boys at this school?"

"Yes, Grandma. There will be boys."

"That's wonderful, sweetheart. Now, I want you to listen to your grandma. This is very important. When you go to class, put on a little red lipstick. Wear high heels. These things matter. Even Marilyn Monroe needed a little help. You know you are no ordinary thing. Who could drive a car like you did at sixteen? You're going to find a husband who is something out of this world. When you put on a little red lipstick, they could call you from Hollywood to be in the pictures."

And with that, I bit into a cinnamon bun, thoroughly enjoying the bewildered faces staring at me.

If I had to pinpoint the moment when I came into myself, this might have been it.

* * *

That was September 1991. I was a young, twenty-year-old living in Cambridge, Massachusetts (having just graduated from college a year early and proceeding straight to law school). My grandmother, whom I knew by her married name, Marion Zornberg—an incredible beauty and live wire in her day—was now a widow in her eighties, living in her one-bedroom rental apartment on Ocean Parkway in Brooklyn. She was my last living grandparent. She was lonely but vital, fierce as a hornet's nest. And funny.

Back then, I don't think I gave ten minutes' thought to how Marion and my other grandparents had laid the groundwork for my own life—I mean *really* laid the groundwork for my life, by immigrating to this country. How all four of my grandparents, each with his and her own story, left Europe in the early 1900s as part of the great migration of Jews rushing to leave wars and pogroms and poverty in Eastern Europe to start over in America. How they got on steamships, vomited their way across the Atlantic in steerage, learned English, and earned their citizenship so that they and their children, and their children's children, could have a stab at a better life. My grandparents loved America with a dearness and a brand of patriotism derived from knowing that where they had come *to* was way better than where they'd come *from*.

My grandmother hadn't put much stock in my attendance at Harvard, I guess, because it didn't seem relevant to the daily America she lived. But to me, that I was able to attend Harvard— that esteemed bastion of American universities—two generations after Marion stepped off the boat as a poor, non-English-speaking newcomer, is part of my experience of the American dream.

As I sat in Dean Clark's office that September morning, I must have sensed that access to my grandmother's world was disappearing. Not long after, I began making sure I called Marion from law school at least once a week. The conversations didn't last long. Just long enough to "change a word," as she would say. Marion would tell me about her ailments, her loneliness, and then she'd ask, with a spark in her voice, whether I'd found a husband yet. I jotted down snippets of our chats, shoving those scraps of notes into a black binder, where they have been sitting these last twenty-five-plus years. Snippets like the following.

Going out on a date

Lisa: Grandma, it's Lisa. I have some news for you.

Marion: So what are you waiting for?! This is what I'm living for. Maybe some good news will pick me up and now I'll be able to see on my eye.

Lisa: I have a date tomorrow night with a new guy.

Marion: Oh yeah? Is he tall?

Lisa: Not very. Maybe about five-foot-seven.

Marion: Okay, so why do you need a six-footer? So you should come up to his pocket? Tell me, is he a doctor?

After a breakup with that guy

Marion: Look, just because an apple looks beautiful on the outside doesn't mean it's going to taste any good. Just this afternoon I cooked a gorgeous yam for lunch. Beautiful orange color. I took one bite and, feh, I had to throw it right in the garbage. This fella you just ended things with isn't worth a darn thing. I'm telling you, his mother is probably a scoundrel. Don't worry, you'll find someone outstanding. And I'm just waiting for you to find a nice boy so I can die. Do you understand, darling?

On a hot day

Lisa: Grandma, isn't it hot in your apartment?

Marion: I have that fan in the kitchen. It's like standing in a Frigidaire.

* * *

Marion died in September 1995, the year after I graduated from law school. Writing this story now, in 2019, I am forty-eight years old and I have a wonderful husband (and he's a doctor!) and two children of my own. It has been nearly one hundred years since Marion crossed that great ocean on a steamship from Europe. And it is time to give voice, as best as I can, to her life and journey, for they are the bridge to my own.

My grandmother, Marion Zornberg, did not attend Harvard. I did. But in ways more tangible than factual truth, she was there with me the whole time. These are her stories.

But Wait! The Making of a History Detective

Something thrilling happened when I started to research this book. For all the stories that Marion had told over the years, I discovered that her early life and coming-to-America story were more mystery than memoir.

Oh sure, I knew stories of the Marion who came of age in Brooklyn during the Roaring Twenties; who worked for a bootlegger during Prohibition and won a Charleston dance competition in the Catskills. I knew of the singing and dancing Marion who clearly missed her calling as an actress, and who had dozens of suitors. "Marion, give us a smile!" they begged her, so they could admire her dimples and pearly whites. And, I knew of the Marion who ultimately chose to marry Emanuel Zornberg, my grandfather, a fellow immigrant from her same Eastern European hometown, not because Emanuel had wealth or prospects but because he was smart and wrote more beautifully than anyone she'd ever met. Finally, I knew of the Marion who worked hard at various jobs throughout her life—"strong like an ox," as she described herself—and who cooked like nobody's business.

But the Marion who grew up in Eastern Europe and immigrated to America? *That* Marion was a mystery. It turns out that no one in the family knew Marion's true birth name—first or last—or when she was born, or how old she was when she left Europe with her family, or—most riveting of all—the *crazy, fascinating* truth about how Marion and her brother, Hymie, and sister, Ruth, and their parents, Sarah and Meyer, managed to enter the United States in 1922 after they were ordered excluded upon arrival at Ellis Island and thrown into detention to await a ship back to Europe. All we were told by Marion is this: The family was saved by an aunt from the Bronx who spoke "a perfect English," and that this aunt supposedly took a train ride down to Washington, DC, where she supposedly met with President Calvin Coolidge personally and persuaded Coolidge to let her family into America. Surely this was just a legend, but could it possibly have a basis in fact? No one knew.

These mysteries propelled me on a journey of my own, a historical journey through ship manifests, census records, 1920s newspapers, nineteenth-century Polish birth records, New York City cemeteries, and Ellis Island, all of which led me, ultimately, to the US National Archives. Let me tell you, it is remarkable how much history one can learn, and how much original research one can do these days sitting at a kitchen counter, armed with a laptop, the internet, and a healthy curiosity.

It was from the National Archives in Washington, DC, that I received in the mail the most exciting package ever: A treasure trove of records, transcripts, and Western Union telegrams that a clerk had located on some dusty shelf, revealing the lost and hidden facts of Marion's immigration story. It knocked my socks off. The journey of Marion's family to America—the fate of my family—was caught up in a web of 1920s politics, intrigue, and immigration policy. Senators, congressmen, power brokers, doctors, aid workers, immigration inspectors, and steamship owners all played a role in this tale of determining Marion's destiny, and hence my own. This story is bigger than Marion. It is the story of a critical period in American history and changing American immigration policy, told up close in microcosm. It is part of this nation's fabric. And many of the same themes that informed Marion's story still resonate today, one hundred years later. This is all to say that I have finally put my undergraduate degree in American history from Harvard College to good use.

After considering for a long time how best to tell this story, I decided to tell it in two voices. Each chapter begins with Marion's stories told in her own voice as a senior citizen living on Ocean Parkway in Brooklyn. I've channeled my grandmother's language and wit into a first-person narrative, to capture as best I can the essence of her world as she expressed it over the years.

The second part of each chapter is told by me as the history detective, to bring you along on my journey, shovel in hand, digging through the annals of history to unearth and consider the forces that shaped Marion's coming-to-America story, including facts Marion never shared and many others that she surely never knew herself.

Let's begin.

CHAPTER ONE

Life in the Old World

Stories Are Worth More than Diamonds

I AM MARION ZORNBERG AND THESE ARE my stories. True ones. Not the fake stories you see on television, where the men pretend to be superheroes, and women parade around in skimpy clothing, showing off all their merchandise. I never did like watching people's *tuchuses* [rear ends] hanging out. In the 1920s, when I won the Charleston dance competition in the Catskills, I didn't have my tuchus hanging out, and the boys still couldn't keep their eyes off me.

To my grandchildren, and great-grandchildren, and great-great-grandchildren: I am telling you these stories because they belong to you too. They are a part of you. Don't you want to know how you came to be born in America instead of in some dark cave in Europe? Of course you do. Don't you want to know how you came to be born at all? So I am giving you these stories. Read them. Tell them to your own grandchildren. Exaggerate here and there if you want to. There is nothing wrong with a little exaggeration, it is one of the spices of life. I will let you in on a little secret: A person's stories are more valuable

9

than the finest pearls or diamonds in the world. Anyone can buy pearls or diamonds at a store, but your stories belong only to you. No one can make them but you. They are yours to keep, and your stories are what make life worth living. Don't forget that.

My Brother's Stink

I had an older brother, Hymie, and a younger sister, Ruthie. Growing up, Hymie was always a troublemaker. Once, when we were living in Brooklyn already, Hymie made me an offer. "Mirinyu," he said. (That's what he called me in Yiddish). "Here is the deal I have for you. I just made a huge stink from taking a shit. If you go in there, and stay in there breathing in my stink for five minutes, I'll give you a nickel." A nickel was worth something back then.

I wanted that money so badly—you can't imagine how badly—so I took the deal. I went into the toilet (that's what we called the bathroom) and he locked me in. And God help me, that was the WORST stink in the world. The devil himself could die smelling that stink. I thought I would die, honest to God. But I stayed in there for the whole five minutes. And when Hymie finally let me out, after I finally escaped that horrible stink, clutching at my throat for air, I wanted my money. But Hymie laughed. He didn't even *have* a nickel. He was just playing a rotten trick on me.

So you know what I did? I picked up a chair—a wood one—and I cracked it over his head. That's what I did. I was a strong girl and I didn't pause one second. Hymie wasn't laughing any more when our mama took him to the doctor to get stitches in his bleeding head.

My whole life I was very strong. Tough as nails. And I had a touch of crazy running through my veins. You know what that means, don't you? It means there's probably some crazy in your veins too.

My Beginnings

Now, I am going to take you back to the place where I was born. Close your eyes so you can get a picture in your head. Imagine a cave. Not a real cave in the side of a mountain, but a small house made of wood, with a beaten mud floor. A hut. With no toilet, hardly any furniture, a kerosene stove. It might as well have been a cave.

When I think of Europe—a place I left, thank God—this is what I see in my head. This dark hut. This cave.

I was born in the 1900s before the First World War. I can't say for sure in what year, and even if I knew, why should I tell you? I didn't keep track of my age and eventually I forgot it. If anyone asked my age, I told them to mind their own business.

I was born one day in that dark cave to the most loving, wonderful, and deeply religious people in the world, Sarah and Meyer. Sarah and Meyer had a hard life. When they were twenty, they already looked like they were forty.

Here, look at my parents on their wedding day.

Sarah was sixteen years of age in this photo. Can you believe it? On her wedding day, she looked fifty; forget about forty. This was in the 1800s yet. In those days no one smiled for pictures. Maybe because they had bad teeth.

Sarah gave birth to ten children but only three of us survived

11

past infancy: Hymie, Marion (me), and Ruthie. Hymie is a nickname for Chaim, his given name, which means life. That was a good name for the first child born to my parents who survived past a year. And I was the oldest surviving girl.

In Europe, my little sister's name was Ruchel. Try to say it right, in Jewish. Not Rachel, like an American would say it, but Roo-chel. You have to pronounce the "ch" like you're bringing up phlegm from the back of your throat. Try it: Ru-chel. Later, in America, she became Ruth and I called her Ruthie.

Our last name was Scher. So dainty. Don't you think so?

Husiatyn

I was born in the town of Husiatyn, in the part of Europe called Galicia. It was a hard place where Austrians, the Russians, the Poles, and the Ukrainians all competed for power, and where the Jews prayed to be left alone.

Our town was located on the Austrian side of the Zbruch River. To the east, on the other side of the river from us, was Russia. So we lived right on the border between the Austro-Hungarian Empire and the Russian Empire. I was too young to understand it, but the chance of war between Austria and Russia hung over Husiatyn like a suffocating blanket. The Russian Imperial Army could cross the river any time and be on our front doorstep.

The Jews in Husiatyn made a living as merchants, trading with the Austrians and the Russians while praying to God to live in peace. At home we spoke Jewish (which was what we called Yiddish), but we learned Polish too, because the non-Jewish people spoke Polish.

Our house was near a dirt road, near lots of other small huts where our Jewish neighbors lived. When the sun went down and it got dark, that was it, you stayed in the dark. There were no streetlights. In the winter, even if you lit a fire, you were cold. We wore long underwear made of itchy wool all winter long. If you got sick with fevers, you probably died. There were sometimes epidemics of cholera, typhus, and tuberculosis.

This was before the time of cars, before we had indoor plumbing or antibiotics. We had no electricity in the house. To get light, we lit candles or waited for morning.

Sarah and Meyer

Now I will take you back even further, to the 1800s, and tell you about my parents.

My mother's Jewish name was Sura. In English, we say Sarah. Sarah grew up in Husiatyn and her mother was Eidel. Eidel rhymes with ladle. I knew her as Baba Eidel [*baba* is Yiddish for grandmother], the only grandparent I ever knew.

Now listen closely to this next part, because it becomes important to the story later. Baba Eidel was married twice. First, Baba Eidel was married to a man named Green, and she had two sons by him: Jacob and Louis Green. After her first husband died, Baba Eidel went to work in the local *mikvah*, the religious bathhouse, as a mikvah lady, to support the family because she was left alone with two sons. Then Baba Eidel took a second husband, named Weister (pronounced Veyster). After marrying Weister, she gave birth at the age of fifty-two to a girl, my mother, Sarah. Fifty-two! Can you just imagine giving birth at that age? This was about 1880.

So let's review to make sure you are following along: My mother was Sarah Weister, and she had two older, half brothers: Jake and Louis Green. Jake and Louis left for America when Sarah was still a little girl.

My mother, Sarah, was very tall. About five feet, four inches. Oh, you can go ahead and laugh, but I'm telling you that was very tall for a woman back then in Europe. Even most of the men were shorter than that. And Sarah was skinny, like a chicken—skinny and sickly, with asthma. It would have been hard for her to find a husband if she wasn't so kind and such a good cook. Sarah got married to my father at age sixteen. That was the normal age for girls to marry.

Now let's talk about my father, Meyer. He came from a nearby town called Kopyczynce [pronounced Ko-pich-a-nitz]. It was almost next door to Husiatyn. Meyer came from a big family. I don't remember all their names, but he had a twin brother, Rueven, and brothers Yossel and Herschel, a sister named Szprincer, and maybe some others.

Meyer came from a family of butchers. His father was a butcher, his uncle was a butcher, and he and his cousins became butchers. That's how it was for boys. If your father had a trade, you learned the same trade. Hymie, my brother, also became a butcher.

So how did my father, Meyer, come to leave Kopyczynce and go live in Husiatyn? He told us that a rich Viennese man opened a butcher shop in Husiatyn and hired my father to run the store for twenty dollars a week. Such a good man my father was. When he sliced a piece of meat for a customer, it was a thing of beauty. People stood around to watch and say, "Ooh, look at that beautiful meat Meyer sliced." The meat looked so good, you wanted to eat it raw.

Meyer was a clean and religious man. He had kind eyes and wore a beard. He was shorter than Sarah, but not by too much. In their wedding photo I think he must have been standing on a stepstool. Or maybe he put lifts in his shoes.

Back then, to find a husband or wife, a matchmaker introduced the boys and girls. In Yiddish, the matchmaker was called a *shadkhn.*

The shadkhn would look for a good match and if both families agreed, they made a *shidduch,* an arranged marriage. That is how my parents met. The shadkhn paired them and made a shidduch, and everyone in town gathered to give them spoons and dishes as wedding gifts. They were now husband and wife. Meyer was twenty years old and cut meat. Sarah was a skinny, sixteen-year-old asthmatic, and the best cook. These were my wonderful parents.

The Cat's in the Cradle

Sarah and Meyer had a hard life in Europe. Seven of their ten children died in the cradle as babies. Oh, did I tell you that already? Well, some things are worth repeating. Sarah believed that her babies died in the cradle because a cat must have snuck into the house at night from the street, sat on the baby's head, and sucked out its breath. That's what superstitious women believed in those days.

My mama was deeply superstitious, and cats were the worst kind of luck around babies. If you ask me, I think the babies died because, back then, parents used to chew the babies' food before feeding it to the babies. Maybe my parents were passing along germs and didn't know it.

Every time Sarah lost a baby, she lost some of herself too. She was skinny as a pencil. When she wheezed, you thought she might break in two. Maybe when you bury so many of your children, it just becomes hard to breathe.

Of course, we were a religious family, like our Jewish neighbors in Europe. We followed our *rebbe* [rabbi] and all the rules of *Shabbos,* and *kashrut* [being kosher], and the mikvah. Every morning my father put on *tefillin* [Jewish prayer garments] and *davened* [prayed]. He had a beautiful singing voice. My mother wore a *sheitl* [a wig] to cover her hair and only dresses, and she went to the mikvah every month. No Jews worked on Shabbos, Saturday, in our town—it was forbidden by Jewish law.

But the truth of it is that I grew up with two religions. The first one was Judaism, and the second was *superstition.* Oh, you have no idea how superstitious the women of Galicia were. My mother had superstitions about everything you can imagine under the sun. Those strict rules were as much a part of our daily life as brushing teeth and eating kosher food. God forbid we broke a rule of superstition, the "evil eye" would get us.

Here are some of the many superstitions we followed:

If you point at the moon, you have to step on your finger.

If you speak about a dead person, pull your left ear.

If you see a black cat, walk around the block.

Never step over a child or he won't grow.

Tie a red string to a baby's crib to keep away the evil eye.

Spit three times when you see a funeral procession go by.

You get used to it, having a sore ear and a bruised finger all the time. My son, Ira, grew to be five foot seven—maybe he would have grown even taller if someone hadn't stepped over him as a child when I wasn't looking.

My Earliest Memory: Praying for Mama in the Cemetery

I left Europe as a young girl, so I have few memories of it. But I do remember that when I was very young, maybe five years old, Mama became very sick one night. Where my father was, I don't know, but Mama sent me out, alone, to find the town doctor. Being that I was the oldest daughter, she trusted me. Age didn't matter. A child of five back then was like a child of sixteen today. In the dark, I walked through the muddy streets until I found the doctor. On my way back home, I decided to stop at the cemetery where my grandmother, Baba Eidel, was buried. I remember that graveyard like I was there yesterday. I prayed by Baba Eidel's grave that she should watch over Mama and help Mama be okay. I was sure the ghosts and demons would rise up and take me, but they didn't. But the cemetery watchman saw me, such a young girl praying by a grave in the dark like that, with my body swaying and my mouth moving. He told all the townspeople of this wonderful act by a little girl. The people of the town talked about it for days. And thank God, my mama recovered.

Eating Raw Onions to Stay Alive

In 1914, the First World War came. I was still a young girl, hanging on my mother's skirts. All of a sudden, war broke out and it was all commotion. Anyone who could leave Husiatyn left. The rebbe left. We left. We took our things and walked on the dirt road to Kopyczynce, my father's hometown, a little over eight miles to the west.

Soon after we left Husiatyn, we heard that the Russians came across the Zbruch River and attacked. Most of the Jewish homes in Husiatyn were burned to the ground, including ours. We lost everything. All the houses were turned to ashes. Rumors were that the Jewish homes weren't burned by the Russians, but by our local Polish and Ukrainian neighbors. There was no going back for us. In Kopyczynce, we moved in with my father's first cousins, Abraham and Elka, and their seven children—Chaim, Leib, Moshe, Abbe, Gedalia, Esther, and Kayla. Even with all those children, they took us in, an extra five mouths to feed. Abraham's father and Meyer's father had been brothers, and Abraham was a butcher, like Meyer. In Kopyczynce, we weren't far from the battles, but we were far enough. At least here, the Russian Army wasn't marching through the streets.

Then my father, Meyer, was drafted into the Austro-Hungarian Army. He was forty years old, but they sent him a draft notice just the same as a young man. The Army was going to send him to work in the coal mines. It was a death sentence. My parents heard that the men sent to the coal mines never came back alive. That place was a hellhole. And here my brother, Hymie, was still a boy, too young to take care of the family. My sister, Ruthie, was a baby. If my father went off with the Austrian Army, that was the end of all of us.

So the day before reporting to duty, my father ate an entire bag of raw onions. He forced himself to swallow one after another, in tremendous pain, tears running down his face and beard. I watched him do it. Then, with his *kishkas* [insides] ripped to shreds and bleeding, he reported to headquarters—sick as a dog, dripping bloody stool. It worked. The Austrian Army officers took one look at Meyer and he already looked half dead. More trouble than he was worth to the Army. So they sent him home to us. After he got home, two weeks he lay in bed with the blood still running out of him. My father survived to take care of his family, but I swear he aged ten more years in that one day. We spent the next years trying not to get killed during the war, and hoping to get out of Europe altogether.

During the war, my father worked in Abraham's butcher shop in Kopyczynce, while Mama and Hymie made trips on foot to buy flour and tobacco to sell at the local market. Hymie also ran cigarettes back and forth to the Army men to make a few more dollars. That's how our family earned scraps to live on through the war. Communications with the outside world were cut off.

Even in such a crowded house with so many of our cousins, Hymie and I were still the loudmouths of the family. My mother used to ask how two children could make so much noise. Hymie, that rascal, was always teasing. Hymie and I also kept the others entertained with jokes and singing. And my little sister, Ruthie, four years younger than me, was a living doll, always. She was my best friend, my whole life.

Cousin Elka Becomes a Widow

In 1918, our cousin, Abraham, died. It was a great sadness. The war was still going on. Abraham took sick and that was it; his time was up. To make matters worse, his wife, Elka, was pregnant with their eighth child when he died. Poor cousin Elka. She gave birth to a girl, named Etka, after Abraham passed. Baby Etka came into this world during the war, practically an orphan already.

"Now You Live in Poland"

The war finally ended in 1918. "Now you live in Poland," we were told. Just like that. The Austrian Empire was done, finished. New countries were being created from the dust.

My parents tried to get us out of Europe. Remember how I told you that my mother had two older brothers living in America—Jake and Louis Green—Baba Eidel's children from her first husband? Well, Jake had done well in America. And somehow he was able to exchange letters with my mother. I don't know who started it or how they found each other. But eventually they hatched a plan, and Uncle Jake sent money to bring us to America.

The Oldest Girl

To be honest, maybe I remember so little of my life in Europe because I blacked it out. Or because I was too young to remember. When I got to America, I was still a young girl of six or seven, and they put me in kindergarten. The few memories I have—of praying in the graveyard, and how we survived the war—I have told you. I did learn to read in Europe. Even during the war, I had some schooling and could read and write in both Jewish and Polish.

But mostly I helped my mother with the cooking, the cleaning, and watching after Ruthie. As the oldest daughter, this was my job. Times were different and the oldest girl in the family was expected to do most of the housework. I didn't mind, especially since Mama wasn't well a lot of the time.

My mother's cooking was like magic, and I learned at her knee. From crumbs and a little oil, she could make things that tasted out of this world. I learned from her how to roll out the dough to make potato *pierogen, kreplach,* and *blintzes.* And to grind fish and meat, and to make the cheapest and toughest pieces of meat taste delicious. Even from a cow's foot, which cost pennies, I learned to make a delicious meal, *picheh.* And I learned to make a chicken fricassee that, after one bite, you would think you died and went to heaven. And to bake salty *pletzelach* with burned onions. And to make a sweet borscht from beets, and a potato soup with small little dumplings floating on top. I learned from the best. Mama cooked better than anyone on this earth.

For as long as I can remember, I worked hard helping my mother. Take it from me, to be useful is the best thing. Better to be strong and working than sitting home on your tuchus. Later in America, I worked at so many different jobs: In the chemical plant, where we made bootleg whiskey in the basement; at Mayrock's home furnishings, where we sold the most beautiful things; in a fancy dress shop; and at a health food store squeezing juices. Later on, I even worked as a lunch lady at Grady Vocational High School in Brooklyn, where I always gave those hungry boys an extra portion. And I worked helping my husband too. Emanuel was a furrier and he would send me from Brooklyn to Manhattan to carry back the animal skins. Two boxes of animal skins I would carry on my shoulder on the subway car, bringing them all the way back to Eastern Parkway. I was strong, like an ox. When my parents were old and sick, I carried them up and down the flights of stairs and changed their dressings and applied ointments. I was half a nurse. My father used to say to me, "Mirinyu, when you were born, if I knew what you would be like, I would have played music in the street."

Ah, but I'm getting ahead of myself! First, I need to tell you how we left Europe and came to America.

Jake, Our Angel

In 1922, Uncle Jake, our angel, sent us money for tickets to sail to New York. We were excited and scared. It was sad to leave the rest of my father's family, especially cousin Elka, a widow, and her eight children. But it was time for us to go.

* * *

ENTER: THE HISTORY DETECTIVE

What's in a Name?

Colum McCann, one of my favorite novelists, wrote in *TransAtlantic* about the American immigrant experience: "In America you could lose everything except the memory of your original name." Well,

21

when it comes to Marion Zornberg, even that was lost, on purpose. None of the family, not a one, knew Marion's true birth name, first or last, and I suspect it was precisely Marion's objective to forget it herself.

Her original name was Mirka Scheer. Here is how I figured it out.

Marion had always said her birth name was Scher, and in America it was. "Such a dainty name," she would say. Yet, in all my searches on ancestry.com, I couldn't find any immigration record for a Marion Scher.

So I asked around. Different relatives speculated that the family's name had been changed at Ellis Island. "Scher was shortened from Scherovna," said one relative. The name was spelled differently in Europe, as "Szer or Sczer," said another.

I kept digging. Finally, after hundreds of "sounds like" searches on ancestry.com, I hit gold with a search for "sounds like Sarah Scher" (Marion's mother). That query pulled up hundreds of records. Sifting through them, I hit upon a ship manifest listing this family of five passengers, traveling from Cherbourg, France, to New York, in September 1922: "Majer Scheer, Sura Blima Scheer, Rachel Scheer, Chaim Scheer, and Mirka Scheer." *Could it be them?* The names seemed close. Meyer was listed as a butcher, Sura Blima as a housewife. The manifest said they had departed from Kopyczynce, Galicia. Closer yet. Reading further, the manifest listed Meyer's nearest relative in Europe as "Elka" from Kopyczynce, and Meyer's intended destination as to live with "Brother-in-Law Jacob Green" in the Bronx. I had found them! Scheer—with a double "e." And my grandmother's first name was *Mirka*. Who knew?

To make sure that Scheer with two "e's" was not simply a typographical error in the ship manifest, I dug further. Through the websites of Polish records hosted by JRI-Poland and JewishGen, I

22

looked for birth, marriage, and death records from Husiatyn and Kopyczynce. Tellingly, I found no records for any Scher or Scherovna in those towns, but I did locate records for Scheer (with two e's) in Kopyczynce, including two records for *Abraham and Elka Scheer*—a birth record for a daughter born in 1901, and a death record for a son of theirs who died in 1902 at the age of five. Later, records I tracked down from the National Archives showed that Meyer Scheer had a brother, Joseph, who had continued to use the surname Scheer after coming to New York. And finally, once I'd determined Marion's original name, I was able to find her US naturalization records. Sure enough, those papers confirm that she immigrated to the United States in 1922 under the name Mirka Scheer, information she apparently shared with no one but the immigration authorities.

One mystery solved. My grandmother started life as Mirka Scheer and the family's original surname, even in Polish, was spelled Scheer.

Marion's Birthdate

I've given up on nailing down exactly when Marion was born. An impossible task, as nearly every official and unofficial document contains a different birth year. Some of this was surely her own doing. The best I can say is that Marion was born sometime between 1907 and 1911, probably in 1907. Hymie, her older brother, was born in 1903 according to his naturalization papers. Ruth was younger than Marion, born about 1913.

This much is clear: Marion was *way* older than six years old when she arrived in America in 1922, as she had claimed. She was probably fifteen. Her oft-repeated story of arriving in America as a young girl was simply inaccurate.

Marion's Birthplace: A Brief History of Husiatyn

So what do we know of Marion's birthplace, Husiatyn (sometimes spelled Gusyatin)? Husiatyn's Jewish community spanned more than 500 years, and I will tell you about it. But I warn you, there is no happy ending here.

First, let's place Husiatyn geographically. It is small town that still exists today in what is present-day Ukraine, alongside the Zbruch River. Back in the early 1900s, this border town marked the easternmost outpost of the Austro-Hungarian Empire. Husiatyn sat on the west bank of the river, and on the right bank, a mere stone's throw away, sat Imperial Russia. So this is where two empires met, in Husiatyn.

Husiatyn was part of Galicia—a province with as tortured a history as any on the globe. This map of Europe shows the province of Galicia marked in bold:

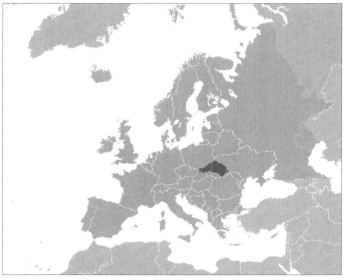

Galicia highlighted on map of Europe. Wikimedia Commons

And in this next rendering of Galicia, you can see that Husiatyn was Galicia's easternmost town, with the Zbruch River marking the eastern border. (The line down the middle reflects the current-day division of Galicia, with the western half part of Poland, and the eastern half of Galicia part of Ukraine.)

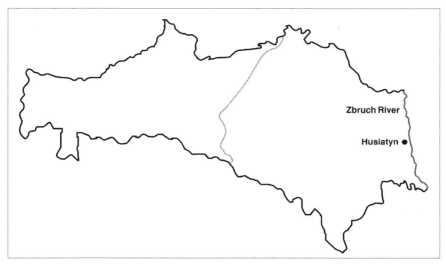

Galicia, 2019, showing current-day division of region between Poland (left) and Ukraine (right). Adapted http://ww.torugg.org

At one time called the "Kingdom of Galicia," Galicia was a poor, underdeveloped region, the control of which changed hands repeatedly between the sixteenth and twentieth centuries. It's hard to keep track of who occupied Husiatyn when. Roughly, Galicia (in parts or in whole) went from the Poles in the sixteenth century to the Ottoman Empire for a decade in the 1600s; then back to the Poles' then to the Austrian Empire in 1772, when Poland was partitioned; then French statesman and military leader Napoleon Bonaparte got in on the action when France briefly seized control of parts of Galicia during the Napoleonic wars; then to Russia in 1807 (as part of the

Treaty of Tilsit); then back to Austria in 1815 (as part of the Congress of Vienna), where it remained under Austrian rule until the First World War; then certain parts went back to Russia, which seized and occupied Husiatyn in 1914; then to Poland after the war; then to the Ukrainians, briefly, in June 1919 (during an insurgency by Ukrainian nationalists); then back to Poland; then to the Germans, who seized control during the Second World War; and to the present-day split of Galicia between Poland and Ukraine (with Husiatyn in Ukraine). You get the idea. The Jews of Husiatyn were polyglots as a survival mechanism.

Jews had settled in Husiatyn in the 1500s. They built this extraordinary sixteenth-century "fortress synagogue" in the Renaissance style.

Jewish fortress synagogue, circa 1920s. Alter Kacyzne, Forward Archives

Perhaps this is where the Scheer family prayed. Jewish photojournalist Alter Kacyzne, who took this photograph in the 1920s, described Husiatyn thus: "A border city in eastern Galicia. The synagogue . . . stands on a hill and is the last building in town. The small white houses in the distance are [over the border] in the USSR."

(By 1922, the Russian empire was called the USSR, the Union of Soviet Socialist Republics.)

Anti-Semitism in Husiatyn was a perpetual problem. Over the centuries, the town's Jewish population was attacked on and off by Cossacks, peasant gangs, and different armies. Depending on who was in charge of the region, Jews were more or less restricted from certain trades, and generally could not own land or participate in government.

But things had looked up for the Jews of Husiatyn under Austrian rule. In 1867, the progressive Austrian government gave equal rights to all social groups, including Jews, as part of the Enlightenment movement. The Austrian constitution abolished restrictions connected with religious observances and granted universal equality before the law. To their delight, Jews were now emancipated citizens. And while they still had to contend on the local level with anti-Semitic neighbors, Jews gratefully experienced increased stability, religious autonomy, and even participation in municipal politics in the fifty years that preceded the First World War.

By 1890—when Marion's mother, Sarah Weister, was coming of age in Husiatyn—Jews comprised two-thirds of this river town's 6,000 residents, and the town was thriving as a regional hub for commerce. It was not a particularly industrialized place (indeed, the Austrian government was unwilling to invest in the industrialization of Galicia precisely because it was an insecure border province), but the townspeople of Husiatyn engaged in dynamic trade with neighbors on both sides of the river, and the town had factories, steel mills, tanneries, and shops.

While most people in Husiatyn were extremely poor, by all accounts the town was spiritually and intellectually rich. Husiatyn was a center of Jewish life in Galicia. The prominent Hasidic rebbe Israel Friedman presided in Husiatyn in the late 1800s and early 1900s, and a Hasidic *beit din* (Jewish court of law composed of rabbinic judges) was established in the town in 1861.

Marion spent too little of her youth in Husiatyn to have had a detailed memory of it. And so deep was Marion's dislike of her time in Europe that she never uttered a kind word about either Husiatyn or Kopyczynce. She spoke of neither unless pressed. Even then, the only image of Europe she offered to her grandchildren was of darkness—the "dark hut." As a result, growing up, I thought the sun shone brighter in America than it did in Europe. That certainly proved true for the Jews of Europe, metaphorically, if not physically.

But now I'll share a glimpse of Husiatyn through a different pair of eyes—those of Emanuel Zornberg (Marion's future husband, my grandfather), who was born and raised in Husiatyn and wrote about it in his memoir, *An Account of My Memories, 1914–1925*. Emanuel was older than Marion, spent more of his life in Husiatyn than Marion had, and preserved clearer and fonder memories of it. Emanuel was also a deeply intellectual man and a romantic. His firsthand portrait of Husiatyn life just before the First World War is a gem of original source material, and possibly the only such account that survives. Here is how Emanuel described Husiatyn:

> It was quite a big town. . . . It was predominantly Jewish; the rest of the people were divided between Poles and Ukrainians. The two minority groups were politely anti-Semitic, but we managed to be friendly, as well as we could. . . . We went to the same schools, and we spoke their language. . . . The Jews were the business people, the non-Jews were the farmers; they had the granary, the Jews had the finished products, a fair exchange.

The town of Husiatyn was a nice place to live in. It was surrounded by very high and very beautiful Russian Mountains. The River Zbruch separated the two countries. The people from each side of the river could see and greet each other. The two countries were not very much infatuated with each other; nevertheless they had friendly relations with one another. The border was open, and there were tremendous commercial activities, exporting and importing. Day and night, Russian transports carrying goods of every description were passing into Austria from which it was shipped by railway to all parts of Europe. Both towns had the same name (on both sides of the river) only ours was the larger one. . . .

The River Zbruch was hundreds of kilometers long, and meandered round and about our town, which made it look like a semi-circle, swimming past the mill and a very long meadow, turning left past the hills upon which the Grand Rabbi's estate expanded. The River went parallel with the beautiful view of outstanding, attractive gardens with trees and flowers. Down below the hill was an area of equal attraction, a romantic place where boys and girls met on Saturdays and Holidays, romancing.

Emanuel offered this further description of Husiatyn's intellectual life:

By the standards of other towns in the vicinity of the same size, Husiatyn was quite progressive in cultural developments. We had a gymnasium, a commercial high school, Yeshivot, a Hebrew School, a court of law, a hospital and doctors. There were a number of factories and many business establishments where people were employed. Particularly important was the importation of eggs from Russia, which employed hundreds of young men, who as a result founded a strong union with modern principles for security and sick benefits.

There was quite an intelligentsia. There were about a dozen Batei-midrashim (synagogues). Most significant was the Zionist movement. The influence of the Haskalah, the new Renaissance, blew in with the winds from the Jewish literati from Russia on one side and from German and Polish culture with which the Jews had been flirting so much. The works of Schiller and Heine were to be found on every Jewish table where there were boys and girls.

Emanuel Zornberg had also grown up admiring and supporting the Austrian kaiser, for the kaiser's liberality and religious tolerance. Emanuel expressed his feeling this way:

Under the Austrian regime, the Jews enjoyed the same equality and rights as other citizens. . . . Kaiser Franz Joseph was a good Catholic, and was very liberal. In certain areas, we practically enjoyed religious autonomy, i.e., the Rabbi had the authority to regulate marriage and divorce. If two people came to him to resolve a religious dispute, his verdict was binding. One could go home with the tallis on his shoulders on Saturday, and nobody would bother him. My father was serving in the Kaiser's army for three years, fought in his war and prayed to God for his life. The Jews across the border [in Russia] didn't have these freedoms. They had pogroms.

But if the Jews of Husiatyn experienced a relatively golden period in the late 1800s and early 1900s, that ended with the First World War. Following the assassination of Archduke Franz Ferdinand in June 1914, the armies of Europe mobilized. On August 6, 1914,

Austria declared war against Russia. Within days, the Russian Imperial Army answered by crossing the Zbruch River and attacking Austria through Husiatyn. Jewish residents scattered. Fires in town destroyed more than six hundred houses and buildings—most, if not all, Jewish-owned. Many believed those fires had been set not by the invading Russians but by local neighbors, the Ukrainians and Poles, whose anti-Semitism was now less polite.

With the outbreak of war, the Scheer family left Husiatyn for Kopyczynce, never to return. Meyer Scheer narrowly avoided the draft into the Austrian Army by eating that bag of raw onions, as the story goes. Meanwhile, Emanuel's father, Isaac Zornberg, fought in the war as a soldier, under the Austrian flag, while his wife and six children (including Emanuel) evacuated to Chorostkov, another neighboring Galician town.

Thus, both Mirka (Marion) and Emanuel—these future spouses, my future grandparents—were refugees in their youth, driven out of Husiatyn by the First World War.

When the Russian Army finally retreated from Husiatyn, some Jews returned. But they were plagued by peasant gangs and the Ukrainian "soldiers," who filled the void following the war. Pogroms against the Jews of Eastern Europe sharply escalated. Emanuel Zornberg's family experienced the violence firsthand. In 1918, Emanuel's father, Isaac, home from fighting in the war, took his family back to Husiatyn, hoping to rebuild a life there on top of the ashes. (Isaac was a butcher by trade, just like Meyer Scheer.) The results were disastrous. Soon after returning, a gang of Ukrainians abducted Isaac from his store and beat him nearly to death. As recounted by Emanuel in his memoir: "Four bandits with rifles grabbed him [Isaac], threw him into the truck and carried him off. . . . The bandits put him on the tracks, two soldiers were sitting on his head and two on his feet and two gave him twenty-five lashes with a very heavy lash." Then those Ukrainian bandits extorted a ransom payment of 2,000 kronen from the Zornberg family before returning Isaac, a bloody pulp. Isaac survived the beating but never fully recovered. The Zornberg family immediately left Husiatyn for the second time in five years, this time never to return.

By 1921, the Jewish population in Husiatyn had declined to 368. Is it any wonder why? Still, those who remained could not have predicted the utter decimation of the Jewish population that would be completed by the Germans in 1941. On July 6, 1941, the German Army conquered Husiatyn and the Nazis' first act, reportedly assisted by locals, was to attack the Jews. According to historical accounts, 200 Jews were rounded up and shot to death in Husiatyn that day. In March 1942, the remaining Jews of Husiatyn were deported to labor and death camps.

Thus ended 500 years of Jewish civilization in Husiatyn. A dark cave, indeed. A Yizkor (remembrance) tombstone dedicated to the Husiatyn Jews killed by Nazis sits in Israel.

It reads: "In eternal memory of the righteous of the Husiatyn community and the surrounding area (near the Zbruch River) (Eastern Galicia) who perished in the years of the Shoah [the

Holocaust]. Memorial day is the eleventh day of Tammuz. Remembered by people in Israel and the Diaspora whose place of origin was Husiatyn."

As best I can tell, the Husiatyn of today is sparsely populated, with barely a trace of the Jewish life that once existed there. The fortress synagogue stands as an abandoned ruin.

Kopyczynce

Kopyczynce is where Meyer Scheer grew up and where the Scheer family took refuge during the First World War. The town, now called Kopychyntsi, still exists in present-day Ukraine.

In the early 1900s, Kopyczynce was a slightly bigger town than Husiatyn, boasting a population of about 7,100, of which nearly one-third was Jewish. During the First World War, that population swelled with displaced refugees. Kopyczynce was mostly undamaged by the war and was never invaded by Russia. It remained under Austrian control until the war ended, at which time it was declared to be part of Poland.

Anti-Semitism was a problem in Kopyczynce, just as it was in Husiatyn, with a significant spike in violence against Jews immediately after the war. Amid this violence, the Zionist movement, advocating for a Jewish state in Palestine, took strong hold in Kopyczynce in the 1920s. Many Jews left for Palestine, while many others, like the Scheers, left for the United States.

Meyer's cousins in Kopyczynce—the widow Elka Scheer and her eight children—were among those who stayed. Before the war, Abraham and Elka had done well for themselves in the town and were considered to be prominent townspeople. They ran two butcher shops in the town, one kosher and one nonkosher, which Elka and her children continued to operate after Abraham's untimely death. Maybe Elka felt their local prominence and solid livelihood would keep them secure. Or maybe Elka, a widow with eight children, saw no realistic path for leaving. Two decades later, when the Nazis descended on Kopyczynce, Marion would have to wait an ocean away to learn the fate of her dear cousins.

☎

A Telephone Call: October 1991

Marion: [*In Brooklyn, in her one-bedroom rental apartment on Ocean Parkway*] I have to tell you, Lisa, I was at your parents' house yesterday, not for long, just from 4:30 to 6:30 to break the monotony, and I almost died from the frankfurter. Your mother didn't cook it enough. It must have been in the house for five years. But look, I don't say anything. I know she gets home late from work, and I don't go over there for the food—just to change a word. But when I came home, I thought your father would have to take me to Coney Island Hospital. I almost died from it.

Lisa: [*In Cambridge, in my law school dormitory*] Grandma, that's terrible.

Marion: So tell me something new. Are you meeting any nice fellows? If you found someone now, I'd make you the whole house. Lisa, you don't have a better friend in the world. I talk to God about you and ask that he should bring you good things. And when I go into the bathroom, I say, please, God, make sure that I don't fall in the toilet. And if I don't fall in, I say thank you.

35

CHAPTER TWO

Journey to America

From Poland to France

I N 1922, UNCLE JAKE, OUR ANGEL, sent us money to come to America, to come live in New York. Oh, how we celebrated and cried! Then we stuffed our valises and left Kopyczynce for good. The five of us—my parents, Hymie, Ruthie, and me—clinging together like peaches. The hardest part was leaving our wonderful cousins, Elka and her eight fatherless children, who housed us during the First World War. They were like brothers and sisters to us. They prayed for us to have safe passage.

Our ship, the SS *Berengaria,* was scheduled to sail for America on September 12, 1922, from the port of Cherbourg, France. First we traveled by locomotive to Warsaw where my father arranged for our passage. We lived there in Warsaw, in a rented room, until our papers were in order. From there, we loaded our valises onto a bus and headed to France to meet our ship.

I had never been on a locomotive before. Or a bus. Or a boat. Or to a port. Or to any place outside our little section of Galicia. I had never before seen an ocean.

Oh, What a Sight!—The SS *Berengaria*

When we arrived in Cherbourg, France, our eyes were open wide like saucers. Cherbourg was a bustling place, a sea of kerchiefs and bearded men. Thousands of people milled around the streets, speaking different languages. Many were like us—Jews from Galicia speaking Yiddish. Others spoke French, Italian, Polish, Lithuanian. So many people preparing to cross the Atlantic.

The air crackled with energy. How can I describe it to you? Let me see. . . . Ah! . . . There's a dish I make—cheese kreplach. It's like a dumpling made of soft dough, filled with sweet farmer's cheese. Delicious, something out of this world. To serve it, I would I fry up bits of stale bread in butter to go on top. Once that stale bread met the butter in the hot pan it would make a crackling sound. Just hearing it, your mouth would start to water with anticipation. That was what Cherbourg was like, how the air crackled with anticipation.

The steamships—what a sight! Big ships we saw lined up in the port, rising into the sky. Each ship looked like its own city, with giant black smokestacks. Our ship, the SS *Berengaria,* was the biggest of them all. It was black like charcoal and had three stacks. A monster. Look, here is a photograph of the *Berengaria.*

Ruthie and I squeezed each other's hands. Hymie and my father took short haircuts. My mother prayed the boat wouldn't sink like the *Titanic.* Even in Galicia we all heard that story—how ten years earlier, the *Titanic,* supposedly the greatest ship ever built, sank like a rock after hitting an iceberg. In case you didn't know, the *Titanic* had also picked up passengers in Cherbourg, France.

Boarding the *Berengaria*

Getting on that big ship was no easy or quick thing. Oh, sure, the wealthier passengers, the ones who had first- and second-class tickets, waltzed onto the boat like Queen Elizabeth. They settled into private cabins on the upper decks, ate in special dining rooms, sat under parasols, and waited like royalty for the ship to pull away from the dock.

But for us steerage passengers, who had the cheapest tickets, boarding was different. We would be sleeping on the lower decks in the belly of that big ship. We had to arrive at the port a full day early. Why so early? So that the ship company's doctor could look us over like chickens at the market before allowing us to board. He checked us for diseases, rashes, lice. He looked at our heads, our eyes. Another worker for the ship washed down our valises with disinfectants.

Then we had to wait in a long line of people for hours until the ship's officer, who sat with a big black book in front of him, called to us to check over our papers and ask us questions about going to America. So many questions he asked of my father. Where did we come from? Where were we going? Who was our closest relative in New York? Could we read and write? All the answers my father gave, and the man took them down in his big book. Finally, they let us on the boat.

Looking Forward

We sailed on September 12, 1922. It was a Tuesday. The steamship's engines roared to life, and the captain blew the whistle. As we pulled out of the port, the railing was packed shoulder to shoulder, as people stood waving goodbye to Europe. Some people cried. "Thank God and good riddance," that's what I said. I looked forward.

First we sailed to England to take on more passengers in the port of Southampton. Then we began crossing the Atlantic to our new home. I couldn't imagine what New York would be like, but I pictured it in my head being like Cherbourg, all hustle and bustle.

Not one of us spoke a word of English. Uncle Jake was our lifeline now. He was a successful businessman in the garment industry and our future depended on him and our Uncle Louis. And, as Mama kept repeating, New York would certainly need a wonderful butcher like my father, no?

Jake and Louis Green. My mama had not seen her brothers in so many years. Uncle Louis had left Galicia many years before, and Uncle Jake had left even before that, when Sarah was a little girl. I hoped my uncles and their wives and my New York cousins would be nice. I hoped they would teach us to be Americans.

That's Not a Black Cherry!

In steerage, we were squeezed together like grapes. Within five minutes, Mama was already vomiting into a bucket, that's how weak her stomach was. It was a hot September and everyone was seasick from the rocking. We slept in tiny cabins with narrow, steel bunkbeds coming out of the wall, stacked one on top of the next. Between the vomit, the toilet, the engine room, the heat, and the odor coming off people's bodies and spoiled food—feh!—that smell was disgusting. Almost as bad as Hymie's stink. Ruthie and I stayed outside in the fresh sea air as much as possible during the day. The nights were awful.

But there was also so much life on that boat. People from all over. Every morning, the Jewish men davened on the deck in their *tallisim* and tefillin [Jewish prayer garments]. Men played cards. Women sang, people yelled, boys chased girls. Hymie chased girls and caught one. There was laughing, yelling, praying, sweating. I tell you, the whole drama of life played out on that boat.

Ruthie and I made friends with some Italian girls. We communicated with our hands—like playing charades. We acted things out and giggled, trying to guess what the other was saying. And this I'll never forget—one of the Italian girls offered me a fruit. It looked like a black cherry, and I love black cherries. My mother used to make a sour cherry soup that was something out of this world. I took that cherry into my mouth and—*whaaat? That was no cherry!* No, it was my first taste of an olive.

Altogether, the trip across the ocean took nine days. God help us, we couldn't wait to get off that boat. We arrived in New York Harbor on September 20, 1922, a Wednesday. In just two more days, Rosh Hashanah would start. Everyone stood at the railing, excited, as we passed the Statue of Liberty. Now we saw with our own eyes, for the first time, that New York City was a place of the tallest buildings, like out of a fairy tale. Oh, how we looked forward to seeing Uncle Jake and celebrating the Jewish New Year in America. Even more, we looked forward to getting off that awful boat, you can't even imagine how much. It was truly going to be the start of a new year and a new life.

In for the Shock of Our Lives at Ellis Island: Disaster!

At Ellis Island, a nightmare came to life. We were put in detention and ordered sent back to Europe.

Let me tell you what happened. First, after the ship docked in Manhattan, the first- and second-class passengers waltzed off the boat the same way they had waltzed on. If you were rich enough to buy a first-class ticket, or even a second-class ticket, then you were rich enough to live in America and that was that.

But if you were in steerage, like us, we couldn't just walk off the ship. No, first we had to go through more inspection at Ellis Island. And Ellis Island was so crowded that for two whole days more they kept us waiting on the ship, in the harbor. I thought I would die from the waiting. Only then, on Friday morning, September 22, were we allowed to leave the ship and told to load up onto big barges that took us right away to Ellis Island for medical and immigration testing. We went from one boat to another. Now it was *erev* [eve] Rosh Hashanah. At sundown, the holiday would start. Would we get to Uncle Jake in time for dinner? We had no idea but we hoped for the best.

Oy vey ist mir [a Jewish expression, a bit like "Woe is me!"]—If only my father could have bought us second-class tickets, we never would have had the trouble we had. We would have waltzed off the boat into Uncle Jake's arms and that would have been the end of it.

As the barge pulled up to Ellis Island, men in uniform stood at the gangplank, yelling in English: "Men, this way! Women and children, that way! Put your luggage here, drop your luggage here." We didn't know the language, but we shuffled along with the rest of the crowd, my father and Hymie in one line and my mama, Ruthie, and me in another. We lost sight of the men. Then, like long snakes, those lines of people moved into the giant hall at Ellis Island. Watching over us were the doctors, in their dark uniforms and caps. They stared us up and down every twenty feet or so, as we walked and climbed the stairs. When a person looked sick, or had a funny eye, the doctor wrote a code on that person's coat using a piece of chalk, and then that person had to leave the line and go to the medical wing. Mama whispered to Ruthie and me in Yiddish to pinch our cheeks to look pink, and not to cough or sneeze no matter what. In her head, I'm sure she was following every superstition in the book to keep the evil eye away.

Then we reached the doctor who checked our eyes for trachoma. My God, was that painful. Today, trachoma is no big deal—you take an antibiotic and it's gone in a few days. But back then, it was a contagious eye disease that made you blind or dead and no one knew the cure. The doctor pulled my eyelids up and over a big metal buttonhook looking for signs of the disease. Thank God, I didn't have it. Neither did my mother or sister.

We girls made it through the inspection line all right; even Mama did fine. Then we waited for my father and my brother to come. We waited and waited.

They didn't come. My father, Meyer, had been chalked. The doctors at Ellis Island had discovered something not one of us knew until that day—my father had a heart murmur.

What a commotion! The officers told my parents we would have to return to Europe on the next ship. They were keeping us out of America. Until the ship was ready to take us back, they assigned us to dormitories on Ellis Island, separate wards for the men and for the women, where we would sleep.

Go back?! My mother shrieked and pulled her hair out. (Not really did she pull out her hair, but it's an expression to show how beside ourselves we were.) My father was in shock. He looked like he had seen a ghost. There would be no Rosh Hashanah celebration with Uncle Jake and Uncle Louis, no toast to a sweet new year in New York. We were now prisoners of Ellis Island.

Somewhere in that building there must have been a black cat.

ENTER: THE HISTORY DETECTIVE

Putting on Historical Lenses

All right, it's time to take out your historical lenses. I know it sounds corny . . . indulge me. The Scheer journey to America did not happen in a vacuum. The only way to appreciate their transatlantic crossing—and what lay in store for them at Ellis Island—is to view their journey through the lens of history and to size up the political forces brewing at that exact time. You see, when this small-town Jewish butcher and his wife and children boarded the SS *Berengaria* in September 1922, they may have worried about the ocean winds, but the changing political winds were their greater danger.

The Open Spigot—That Is, before It Closed

Are your historical lenses on? Good. First, I want you to picture in your mind a spigot—a faucet—with a strong, plentiful, unrestricted current of water shooting out of it. That is the image of European immigration to the United States from about 1880 until the start of the First World War in 1914. Let's call those thirty-five years the Spigot Years.

It's no surprise that Europeans wanted to move to America in the Spigot Years. The US Civil War was over, the American economy was booming, America was a happening place—the shores of opportunity.

Plus, by the late 1880s, improvements in steamships had made crossing the Atlantic Ocean faster, less dangerous, and less expensive.

America's doors were wide open to European immigrants during the Spigot Years, and Europeans came in droves. (America's doors were not open to Asians, however, during this time, which is another story entirely of rank discrimination). From 1880 to 1914, nearly *20 million* Europeans climbed aboard steamships and arrived on America's doorstep. Most of these new arrivals were poor Southern and Eastern Europeans—peasants from Italy, Russia, Greece, and the vast regions of the Austro-Hungarian Empire (including Galicia)— who were only too happy to leave the feudal vestiges of Europe behind. Ellis Island opened its doors in 1892 to deal with the flow. It was the main immigration processing hub for the federal government, screening anywhere from 2,000 to 5,000 new immigrants per day.

And among those 20 million European immigrants were about two million Jews. What a gift the Spigot Years were for the Jewish people! Indeed, the Jewish community refers to those golden years of immigration as the time of the Great Jewish Migration. America's open-door policy for European immigration allowed the Jews of Europe to leave in mass numbers never seen before or since, escaping centuries of degradation and abuse.

I am telling you this to set the stage—because by the time the Scheers boarded the SS *Berengaria* in 1922, the spigot was actively being shut off. *Luckily* for the Scheers, they squeezed into the last drips of the Great Jewish Migration. *Unluckily* for them, 1922 was a time of sharply changing attitudes, when far fewer Eastern and Southern Europeans were allowed in, and when Ellis Island officials aggressively exercised their broad discretion to keep out those they deemed ineligible for admission.

A Brief (and Riveting!) History of Jews in America Leading Up to 1922

Now let's turn the clock back even further and review, with an even broader lens, the history of Jews in America up to this point, and the pattern of American immigration generally, to get a better sense of the country the Scheers were trying to come *to* in 1922.

Okay, so we all know that the Pilgrims who arrived at Plymouth Rock in 1620 were from England. And, yeah, they were not Jewish. Nope, the American colonies grew mostly out of settlements by Protestant farmers who were British subjects.

But were there any Jewish people in colonial America? Yes, absolutely . . . just in teeny, tiny numbers. Jews in America predated British control, going all the way back to the mid-1600s, when the island of "Manhattan" was still a Dutch settlement governed by Peter Stuyvesant.

By the time of the American Revolution, in 1776, an estimated 2.5 million people lived in the American colonies, of whom about 1,500 were Jewish. That's 0.06 percent of the American population. Like I said, teeny, tiny numbers. Those colonial Jews were mainly Sephardic Jews originally from Portugal and Spain. They or their ancestors had voyaged to the Americas after being exiled during the Spanish and Portuguese Inquisitions. (The Inquisitions were the cataclysmic centuries of Jewish despair, from 1480 to 1834, during which the Spanish and then the Portuguese monarchies ordered Jews to convert to Christianity, leave, or die. Most Jews who left Spain and Portugal moved to other parts of Europe, including Galicia. But some of those expelled Jews risked a voyage to the Americas instead, settling in Brazil, the Caribbean, and the American colonies.)

Curiously, the Puritans of colonial America liked to compare themselves to the ancient Hebrews. And so, as late as 1787, students at Harvard College were required to study Hebrew. Judah Monis, a Jew of Portuguese descent, taught Hebrew at Harvard from 1722 to 1760. His ultimate conversion to Christianity caused a stir among Jews and Christians alike.

About one hundred Jewish men served as patriot soldiers in the American Revolution. You may have heard of Haym Solomon, a Jewish New Yorker of Portuguese descent who famously helped George Washington to finance the Battle of Yorktown, at great personal sacrifice (Solomon died penniless as a result). In the fifth grade, I was cast as Haym Solomon in a school play. My clearest memory of that theatrical experience is being yelled at during rehearsals; to the director's shock and horror, I kept pronouncing the word "comfortable" in a thick Brooklyn accent as "cumf-ta-bull." It was the last time I acted in a play . . . but I digress.

Now let's fast-forward to the nineteenth century. By the year 1800, the total US population had grown to an estimated 5.3 million people, of whom about 2,000 were Jewish. Still fledgling, Jews comprised less than one-half of one percent of the US population. Take a guess: Where would you find the largest Jewish American community in 1800? Answer: Charleston, South Carolina. Yes, Jewish Southerners! Most of those early Jewish Americans lived in Charleston and Savannah, with other small clusters in New York, Newport, and Philadelphia.

But change was afoot on America's population landscape and also for the Jewish American population. Between 1820 and 1870, the young country saw its first huge influx of immigrants—from Germany and Ireland. In that fifty-year span, nearly 7.5 million

German and Irish immigrants sailed to America—doubling the size of the US population—and included in that wave were roughly 150,000 German Jewish immigrants. The Irish immigrants were escaping famine; indeed, as much as one-half of the entire Irish population left Ireland to come to America. The Germans (or Bavarians, as southern Germans were then known) were escaping revolution and poverty. The German Jewish immigrants were additionally escaping anti-Semitic German laws that increasingly restricted Jewish men from working in trades or legally marrying. Often, those young Jewish men came over by themselves at first, found a way to make a living in America, and then went back to Germany in order to return to America with their relatives and a girl to marry.

Was it easygoing for the Irish and German immigrants of the mid-1800s? Hell, no. The conditions for crossing the Atlantic were dismal and many died of disease on what became known as "coffin ships." Beyond that, the US populace has always had its share of ugly prejudice. Brutal white-on-black racism was a dominant feature of American society, with the population of enslaved blacks reaching 3.9 million by 1860. Meanwhile, the large influx of European immigrants that began around 1820 kicked up white-on-white prejudice, premised on religious and cultural differences. Irish Catholic immigrants had to contend with the fierce wrath of the anti-Catholics, who branded the Irish Catholics a subhuman race and portrayed them as lazy—and yet also as in America to steal all the good jobs. Nativist groups, advocating for anti-Catholic policies, formed in cities across America and even formed a political party (the Know Nothing Party), which gained some prominence in the 1840s and 1850s. German immigrants (non-Jewish and Jewish) faced prejudice because they spoke a foreign language, a blot on the

Anglo-Saxon character of the country. Jewish immigrants additionally contended with the grotesque stereotype of the Jew as Shylock, a Jewish moneylender portrayed as a loan shark in *The Merchant of Venice*. And yet, notwithstanding the prejudices in some quarters, America absorbed all these European immigrant newcomers like a thirsty sponge, putting them to work building canals and railroads, settling vast empty farmland, increasing commerce, and otherwise fueling the American Industrial Revolution.

The arrival of 150,000 German Jews in the mid-1800s exponentially increased the Jewish population in America. And let me tell you something else about this wave of Jewish immigrants: They were rock stars, in my opinion. Those German Jewish immigrants fanned out across America, establishing communities and businesses not only in New York, Philadelphia, and Boston, but also in Chicago, Cincinnati, Baltimore, Kansas City, and San Francisco. They were merchants, haberdashers (clothing makers), and store owners. Many began as peddlers with large sacks strapped to their backs, later using horses and buggies, as they took dry goods from the cities to remote agricultural areas. Within a short space of time, they had built and built and built: Not just families, but also factories, synagogues, hospitals, and philanthropic organizations.

They built infrastructure for Jewish life in America, most of which still exists today. They established B'nai Brith, a Jewish service organization, in 1843, to help care for the sick, the elderly, widows, and orphans. They established the American Reform Judaism movement, a distinctly Americanized form of Judaism, in Cincinnati in 1848. These German Jewish immigrants were secular, literate, and ambitious. Here, in America, they quickly acculturated and sought out educational and professional opportunities from which they had been barred in Europe, entering medicine, science, and law. In commerce and merchant banking, they emerged as respected, risk-taking leaders. The Lehman brothers and the Guggenheims were part of this German immigration wave. So was Marcus Goldman, who emigrated from Germany in 1848 and went from peddler-with-horse-drawn-cart to Philadelphia storekeeper before hanging out his shingle as a merchant banker on Pine Street in New York City circa 1847. He later joined with Samuel Sachs, the son of a Bavarian rabbi, to found the firm of Goldman Sachs.

As historian Howard Sachar put it, in the 1800s "at best, Americans still regarded the Jew with wary curiosity," and in frontier society, there was "not much serious interest one way or the other." German Jewish immigrants forged ahead and embraced American life and democracy in all its regional flavors, the Southern Jews becoming Southerners, the Northern Jews becoming Northerners, and the Western Jews becoming Westerners. By the late 1800s, at least three sizable American cities had elected Jewish men as their mayors: Iowa City, Seattle, and San Francisco.

During the Civil War, Jewish Americans split along the North-South divide, just like their non-Jewish neighbors. The German Jewish population in Chicago was sufficiently large and passionate to raise a complete company of Jewish volunteers to fight for the Union, as part of the 82nd Regiment. Jews of the South, some of whom owned slaves, backed the Confederacy. No central rabbinic authority existed to offer spiritual guidance on the issue of slavery; and of the scant number of rabbis in America, some were abolitionists while others opposed Jewish discussion of the "political issue" of slavery. Of the estimated 10,000 Jews who fought in the Civil War, 7,000 fought for the Union and 3,000 fought for the Confederacy. Coincidentally, Jewish doctors held the rank of surgeon general on both sides of the conflict (David Camden de Leon for the South, and Phineas Horwitz for the North).

Here is where things stood after the Civil War ended: By 1870, the US population had surged to 38 million people. Of that total, about 200,000 Americans were Jewish. So we are still talking about a tiny percentage—Jews remained one-half of one percent of the growing US population—and yet the Jewish community was by this time a recognized religious group in the United States.

And then came the Spigot Years, those peak years of immigration to the United States, from 1880 to 1914, when a deluge of people arrived from Eastern and Southern Europe. Twenty million—a volume that dwarfed any immigration the United States had previously experienced. Whole towns emptied out in Italy, Russia, the Austro-Hungarian Empire, and elsewhere. Two million of those immigrants (about one-tenth) were Jewish men, women, and children.

Something was noticeably different about immigration in the Spigot Years besides the sheer volume. Unlike any prior immigration wave, almost *none* of these newcomers spoke English when they arrived. They spoke Italian, Russian, Yiddish, Polish, Romanian, Hungarian, Greek, Spanish, and Lithuanian. Sweeping into urban centers by the millions looking for work, they brought their European customs and languages with them. Immigrant life was incredibly hard and the majority of these 20 million people lived in poverty in the slums and urban ghettos of American cities. Still, they began planting roots just like their immigrant forebears.

Within the American Jewish community itself, the Spigot Years were not devoid of intra-ethnic tension. The established German Jews of America worried mightily that the entry of so many uncouth, poor, Eastern European Jews would damage the reputation of Jews

51

as a whole and stir up anti-Semitism. A sense of superiority was no doubt at play too, in a culture clash of Western over Eastern Jews; German over Yiddish; uptown over downtown. But by the turn of the twentieth century, as the influx of Eastern European Jews became an undeniable reality—and as violence against the Jews of Russia continued to escalate—the German Jews of America once again responded, determined to embrace their Eastern European cousins.

With an ethos both of philanthropy and of wanting to protect the good name of Jews in America, Jewish American community leaders at the turn of the century impressively mobilized to help with the settlement, absorption, and speedy Americanization of the newer arrivals. Jewish orphanages, settlement houses, medical clinics, and old-age homes all found financing and staffing. The National Council of Jewish Women (NCJW) played an outsized role in protecting female Jewish immigrants who arrived at Ellis Island without guardians and worked to eradicate the sex trafficking trade that ensnared many Jewish girls—including by working to secure passage of the federal Mann Act (criminalizing sex trafficking) in 1910. Other Jewish organizations worked to improve hygiene and conditions in the tenements, and still others—like the Bureau of Social Morals—hired private investigators and partnered with local police and prosecutors to weed out embarrassing pockets of Jewish organized crime that had sprung up in the overcrowded Lower East Side of New York City. By so doing, the Jewish community forged a positive relationship in the 1890s with New York City Police Commissioner Teddy Roosevelt, who later became the first US President to appoint a Jew to his cabinet.

Eastern European Jews too, after settling in America, promptly formed their own social welfare organizations to aid incoming sisters and brothers. HIAS—the Hebrew Immigrant Aid Society—was the most significant, providing immediate help to the many thousands of arriving Jewish immigrants at Ellis Island and other ports of entry. The Educational Alliance sponsored classes to learn English and how to be a good American. The Workmen's Circle, formed in 1900 by Yiddish-speaking immigrants, sponsored lectures, provided life insurance and unemployment relief, and supported the Jewish arts. Thousands of *landsmanshaften*—social groups of Jewish immigrants from the same towns of Eastern Europe—sprang up to provide yet another safety net and outlets for fraternizing and networking.

Truly, one cannot overstate the profound impact of Jewish philanthropy and community building during the Spigot Years of immigration. "No immigrant group in American history ever was taken in hand more solicitously by members of its own community," concluded historian Howard Sachar. By 1917, thousands of Jewish societies, benevolent associations, fraternal orders, and landsman-shaften operated in New York City.

Jacob and Louis Green: Making It in the New York City Garment Industry

Most of the two million Eastern European Jews who arrived during the Spigot Years settled in New York City. They clustered in the tenement houses of the Lower East Side of Manhattan, in awful, cramped apartments. Many found jobs in the garment industry, working in the factories built by their German Jewish predecessors or as street peddlers. Others, bringing skills from Europe, entered trades like watchmaking, bookbinding, and cigarmaking. Still others opened groceries, candy stores, bakeries, and, yes, butcher shops.

But the Jewish garment industry of New York City was *king*. This cannot be overemphasized. During this period of American history, the immigrant Jews of New York City clothed America. The cowboys of the Wild West wore blue jeans designed and manufactured by Levi Strauss (a German Jewish immigrant who had come to America in 1847 to work in his brothers' dry goods business). Upper-crust Protestant ladies in Savannah wore dresses handsewn by Jewish tailors in New York City sweatshops. Here are some mind-blowing statistics for you: By 1910, New York City was producing *70 percent* of the entire nation's women's clothing and 40 percent of its men's clothing. Jews constituted *80 percent* of the nation's hat and cap makers (at a time when everyone wore hats and caps), *75 percent* of its furriers, and *68 percent* of its tailors. If you walked down Essex Street on the Lower East Side in 1920, you would hear 10,000 sewing machines whirring. In the early 1900s, the Lower East Side of Manhattan was the most densely populated place on Earth, and apparently everyone had a sewing machine.

Enter Uncle Jake Green, the older half brother of Sarah Scheer. As best I can piece together, Jake left Galicia by himself for New York in 1889, at the age of seventeen. He probably started out at the bottom as a day laborer in a Lower East Side sweatshop and worked his way up in the garment industry. He must have done fairly well, because nine years later, in 1898, Jake brought over his younger brother, Louis Green, from Europe.

By 1920, both brothers had prospered, thanks to the New York City garment industry. According to the 1920 census records, Jake—forty-nine years old—was a US citizen and owned his own garment business, listing his occupation as "Manufacturer, Clothing Store owner." He was also a family man, married to Mollie Green, with four children: Mona (already married), Morris (age eighteen), Minnie (fifteen), and Harold (seven).

Louis was forty-three years old, a US citizen, and likewise the owner of a "cloak manufacturing" business, according to 1920 census records. He was married to Anna (Annie) Green, a native New Yorker whose parents had previously emigrated from Europe, and they had two children, Mildred (fourteen) and Harold (twelve). (Time out: Who could have imagined that "Harold" was such a popular name in the early 1900s that *both* Jake and Louis named their sons Harold Green. . . . I'm just saying.)

By 1920, Jake and Louis had also risen above the overcrowded, poor conditions of the Lower East Side. They were living in the Bronx—the upwardly mobile section of New York City at that time—on the same street. Jake lived at 903 Tinton Avenue, and Louis lived a block or two away at 1043 Tinton Avenue. With the First World War over, they sought to bring over their half sister, Sarah, whom they had not seen in decades.

What a wonderful and exciting prospect for Sarah, Meyer, and their three kids to be reunited with Jake and Louis in New York City! When the Scheers set sail in 1922, they headed toward what was not only a supportive immediate family, but also an exceptionally vibrant city and community.

Jewish life in America had prospered, with New York City at its epicenter. There were the established Jews who had come over generations before from Germany, and the more recent layer of Yiddish-speaking newcomers around whom the Yiddish theater and dozens of Yiddish newspapers had sprung up—a community bursting with ambition. And common to the layers of Jewish

American life in the early 1920s was pride. Immense, palpable pride in becoming and being American. Think about it in these terms:

By 1922, when the Scheers set sail, Irving Berlin (born in Siberia and raised on the Lower East Side) had written "God Bless America."

By 1922, Louis Brandeis (born to German Jewish immigrants and raised in Louisville, Kentucky) was an associate justice on the US Supreme Court.

By 1922, Julius Rosenwald (the son of German Jewish immigrants) had built Sears, Roebuck and Company into the quintessential American mail-order business.

By 1922, Jewish hospitals were among the leaders in American medicine and had substantially contributed their medical staffs to the US Army Medical Corps hospitals in France during the First World War.

By 1922, Benny Leonard (born Benjamin Leiner and raised on the Lower East Side) was the lightweight boxing champion of the world.

By 1922, the sonnet written by Emma Lazarus (of German and Portuguese Jewish descent) had been emblazoned on the pedestal of the Statue of Liberty: "Give me your tired, your poor, Your huddled masses yearning to breathe free."

By 1922, Morris Michtom, a Russian-born candy shop owner living in Brooklyn, had developed the teddy bear in honor of former president Teddy Roosevelt.

By 1922, artists and sculptors like William Zorach (born Zorach Gorfinkel in Lithuania) and Elie Nadelman (born in Warsaw) were leading a distinctly American art movement embracing Cubism and Modernism.

One more statistic: By 1922, Jews composed just 3 percent of the total US population, and yet Jewish students composed 21 percent of Harvard's freshman class.

This was the vibrant world into which the Scheers were arriving. Jewish immigrants had enthusiastically woven themselves into the fabric of a dynamic nation. But as we shall now turn to consider, not everyone shared that enthusiasm. A backlash was growing.

The Closing Spigot

By the time the Scheers boarded the SS *Berengaria* in September 1922, the tide of popular sentiment had turned and the immigration spigot was being shut. Many Americans—including those elected officials in Congress, with power to legislate—had come to perceive the poor, steerage, foreign-language speaking passengers of Eastern and Southern Europe as "undesirables." Immigration was a great problem to be addressed, not a positive to be celebrated. This wasn't just about the Jews. It was the Italians, Russians, Greeks, Poles . . . the whole lot. In 1917, and then again in 1921, Congress tightened the spigot with restrictive immigration laws aimed at keeping Eastern and Southern Europeans out. The year 1921, in particular, marked a huge shift in American immigration policy when—for the first time in American history—Congress set quotas to sharply reduce immigration from Southern and Eastern Europe. And then in 1924, Congress shut the spigot entirely. The welcome-to-America mat had been officially rolled up and tossed back into the closet.

So, what happened? This country is so magnificent and, at the same time, so complex. While the rosy narrative painted earlier— of Jewish and other European immigrants ambitiously weaving themselves into the fabric of American life—is entirely accurate, it vies with what else was happening in America during those same years. So before we return to the Scheers' story, let's look one more time through our historical lenses to decipher the rising anti-immigration sentiment and forces that made the Scheers' journey in 1922 especially difficult.

The First World War had a lot to do with it. It was a time of nationalistic and nativist fervor. The United States had joined the Allied forces in 1917 and fought *against* Austria-Hungary and Germany. Anti-European feelings flared. After the war ended in 1918, Americans were not keen on taking in an influx of immigrants from regions they had just defeated in a world war. It kinda makes sense, right?

And then there was the rising labor movement in America, which was no friend to immigration. As labor leaders organized and fought for better wages and conditions for American workers, the last thing they wanted was for cities to be flooded with even more poor immigrants willing to take any job at any wage. Even Jewish labor leaders of the time, like Samuel Gompers, supported strict anti-immigration measures.

Other powerful forces were at play too—and I speak now of the American eugenics movement and the Red Scare—two critical drivers of American immigration policy in the 1920s. Let's take a look.

The American Eugenics Movement— The Backlash to the Spigot

Good morning, class. Today we're going to learn about the American eugenics movement—the progressive American movement of the early 1900s that embraced the genetic superiority of Nordic whites and called for the separation and exclusion of inferior races.

Come again, the . . . *what?* I must have been absent from school the day the teacher taught this chapter of American history . . . or maybe the teacher just conveniently skipped over it.

The American eugenics movement preached that people who came from Nordic, Anglo-Saxon stock (in other words, people from Britain and Northern Europe) were genetically superior to all other humans on earth, both mentally and physically. What did the eugenicists want? Separation of the races; forced sterilization of the disabled, poor, and immoral; and strict immigration laws to keep out undesirables—all with the stated goal of improving American destiny by breeding more desirable Americans.

The word eugenic comes from the Greek word *eugenes,* meaning "well-born." This is ironic, considering that American eugenicists deemed Greeks to be among the genetically inferior.

The rise of the American eugenics movement directly coincided with the mass influx of poor immigrants from Southern and Eastern Europe during the Spigot Years. It took root in the late 1880s and came into full swing in the 1910s and 1920s, about the same time as the ascendency of the white supremacist hate group, the Ku Klux Klan. In other words, eugenics was a backlash to the spigot. Old-stock Protestants felt that the recent immigrants who had flooded US cities—Catholics, Jews, non-English speakers—could never be truly American and would bring ignorance, disease, crime, and decline to American society. The eugenics movement validated those beliefs.

What made eugenics especially potent is that it was touted and accepted as an *exact science.* Leading eugenicists—like lawyer Madison Grant, president of the New York Zoological Society—asserted that the mixture of "higher racial types," such as Nordic whites, with other "lower" races had been *scientifically proven* to result in the decline of the higher race. Grant's book, *The Passing of the Great Race,* published in 1916, sold like hotcakes and brought eugenics into the mainstream. Those "inferior races" included blacks, Asians, and all non-Nordic whites. In this supposedly exact scientific thinking, Greeks were a separate "race." Italians, a separate "race." Jews were of the "Hebrew" race, regardless of skin color or country of origin.

The nerve center of the American eugenics movement's research and propaganda was none other than the Cold Spring Harbor Laboratory on Long Island in New York. Now famous for its discovery of deoxyribonucleic acid (DNA) in 1953, the laboratory had its beginnings as a driver of eugenic thought—providing a chilling reminder that "race science" is susceptible to all manner of exploitation. (The Cold Spring Harbor Laboratory, by the way, located twenty minutes from my home, is also where my son, Ethan, attended World of Enzymes camp in 2016. He loved it.).

For Jewish Americans, the rise of eugenic thinking meant their social exclusion from elite circles. Even the wealthiest and most accomplished Jewish Americans found themselves banned from hotels, resorts, and social clubs. The Populist movement, which straddled the end of the nineteenth century and beginning of the twentieth, further stirred anti-Jewish disparagement. Popular literature of the early 1900s, including works by Henry James, portrayed Jews as "swarming" foreign animals. So while, yes, Louis Brandeis sat on the US Supreme Court, one of his fellow justices (James Clark McReynolds) refused to sit next to Brandeis or speak to him for years.

By 1920, under the influence of the eugenics movement, most American states had passed forced sterilization laws of the disabled, mentally ill, and socially marginalized. And politicians embraced the movement's arguments in support of immigration restrictions and bans on interracial marriage.

If the American eugenics movement of the early 1900s sounds eerily similar to policies later adopted by the Nazi regime, and the Nazi plan to create a "master race," that's because it was. When the Nazis came to power in the 1930s, they copied *American* forced sterilization laws and tenets of the *American* eugenicist movement. Thankfully, by that time eugenics had been largely discredited in the United States as more the product of fascism and racism than of credible science. But in the 1910s and 1920s, eugenics was in full bloom in American intellectual circles. It was so mainstream that even African American intellectuals of the day, and academics at Tuskegee and Howard universities, espoused eugenics; except they believed the best blacks were as good as the best whites and that "The Talented Tenth" of all races should mix. Eugenics was taught on virtually every American college campus, including, you guessed it, at Harvard.

Harvard has been called the "brain trust" of the American eugenics movement, reportedly more central to its propagation than any other university in the United States. That is in part attributable to Harvard's president at the time, A. Lawrence Lowell, who presided over the university from 1909 to 1933 and was a big proponent of eugenic policies, including immigration restrictions. Harvard graduates founded the Immigration Restriction League in 1894 to advocate for the "exclusion of elements undesirable for citizenship or injurious to our national character." In 1922, about three months before the Scheers arrived in New York Harbor, President Lowell proposed imposing a 15 percent quota on Jewish students at Harvard. And in that same year, Lowell vigorously enforced a ban on black students living in Harvard's freshman dormitories. (By contrast, Charles Eliot, Harvard's previous president from 1869 to 1909, was a board member, along with Woodrow Wilson, of the National Liberal Immigration League—a nonsectarian organization formed to push back against restrictive immigration policies. Eliot had also championed college admissions based on academic merit, as determined by standardized testing.)

Eugenics unquestionably influenced national immigration policy. In 1911, a congressional committee known as the Dillingham Commission, whose mission was to study the effect of immigration on America, looked to eugenicists as the "experts" on the subject and concluded (unsurprisingly) that heavy immigration from Southern and Eastern Europe posed a serious danger to American society.

In 1917, just as the United States was entering the First World War, Congress overwhelmingly passed the 1917 Immigration Act, imposing a literacy requirement for admission, based on the eugenic belief that "inferior" races had low literacy rates. Going forward, any individual sixteen years or older had to be able to read some language to be allowed entry to the United States. President Woodrow Wilson vetoed this legislation twice. But in 1917, members of Congress from both political parties passed the popular law over his second veto.

The 1917 law also expanded the definition of who could be excluded from entry to the United States on the ground of being "likely to become a public charge"; in other words, likely to become dependent on welfare. Under this revised definition, immigration officials were given broad authority to exclude not just (to use the words of the statute) imbeciles, epileptics, criminals, anarchists, and those with contagious diseases, but also the "poor," "beggars," and "aliens who have a physical disability that will restrict them from earning a living in the United States." Think about that: Virtually every steerage passenger who passed through Ellis Island was poor. It was left to the individual immigration inspector to decide which of those passengers were likely to become public charges and thus to be kept out of the country.

The 1917 law wasn't put to the test until after the First World War ended, when transatlantic crossings became safe again and resumed in 1919. As it turned out, the literacy test was a flop. Way too many Southern and Eastern Europeans could read. (Go literacy!) Massive immigration from Southern and Eastern Europe started back up, surpassing levels of even the years before the war, causing many Americans to freak out.

And Then Americans *Really* Freaked Out: The Red Scare of 1919 and 1920

In 1919 and 1920, a new fear swept Americans: The fear that political radicals—anarchists, Bolsheviks, socialists, communists— were coming to America from postwar Europe to destabilize the US government.

Actual events touched off the hysteria, which became known as the Red Scare. In April 1919, authorities discovered a plot by Italian anarchists to mail thirty-six bombs to prominent members of the US political and economic establishment, including banker J. P. Morgan, oil magnate and philanthropist John D. Rockefeller, Supreme Court Justice Oliver Wendell Holmes, and US Attorney General Alexander Palmer. Most of the bombs were defused without injury, but one bomb—mailed to the Georgia senator who had cosponsored the antiradical Immigration Act of 1918—blew off the hands of the senator's housekeeper and severely injured his wife. Scary stuff.

Then, on June 2, 1919, the anarchists struck again—this time exploding bombs simultaneously in eight American cities. One of the bomb blasts, in Washington, DC, narrowly missed Eleanor and Franklin Roosevelt (then assistant secretary of the Navy). Moments after the Roosevelts had walked past the house of their next-door neighbor, Attorney General Mitchell Palmer, an anarchist on a suicide mission exploded a bomb at the Palmer house. The bomber's body parts landed on the Roosevelts' doorstep. The Palmers were okay, but their house was destroyed.

Then came the Wall Street bombing—the deadliest act of terrorism on American soil up to that time. In September 1920, a large bomb (in a horse-drawn wagon) detonated on Wall Street, at lunchtime, in front of the offices of the J. P. Morgan bank. The blast killed thirty-eight people and wounded hundreds. The Wall Street bombing (one of the earliest terrorism cases investigated by the Federal Bureau of Investigation) was never solved, but it is believed that anarchists were behind that attack too.

The federal government responded to these attacks by arresting suspected political subversives. Known as the Palmer raids, authorities arrested and detained thousands of noncitizens—mostly people from Italy and Russia, including some Jews who favored a leftist form of government. There are disputed accounts about how many of those rounded up were ultimately deported; perhaps about 500, while many arrests were eventually thrown out as illegal. Meanwhile, anti-immigrant sentiment surged to a fever pitch. The prospect of admitting new immigrants from Southern and Eastern Europe at such a time seemed unthinkable to many Americans, a threat to the stability of the United States.

"Whose Country Is This" Anyway?

In February 1921—about eighteen months before the Scheers sailed for America—then Vice President Calvin Coolidge tackled the subject of immigration in an essay, titled "Whose Country Is This?" Published in *Good Housekeeping,* the most popular women's magazine of the day, it is an intriguing piece by the man who would soon become president (after President Warren Harding died of a heart attack in 1923).

In his essay, Coolidge sought to calm anti-immigrant hysteria and reinforce the vital importance of immigration to US prosperity while also stridently agreeing that America had an immigration problem. America should keep its doors open only to "the right kind" of immigration, he wrote. There was certainly no room in America for the anarchist alien— "a danger in our midst"—nor was there room in America for the "weak of body, the shiftless, or the improvident."

Addressing the immigration ideal, Coolidge extolled the example of the Pilgrims and Harvard—there's Harvard again—writing:

The Pilgrims were not content merely to reach our shores in safety, that they might live according to a sort of daily opportunism. They were building on firmer ground than that. Sixteen years after they landed at Plymouth, they and their associates founded Harvard College . . . that was their offering for the common good. It would not be unjust to ask of every alien: What will you contribute to the common good, once you are admitted through the gates of liberty? Our history is full of answers of which we might be justly proud. But of late, the answers have not been so readily or so eloquently given. Our country must cease to be regarded as a dumping ground.

Coolidge then gave a firm nod to the eugenics movement, declaring, "There are racial considerations too grave to be brushed aside for any sentimental reasons. *Biological laws tell us that certain divergent people will not mix or blend. The Nordics propagate themselves successfully. With other races, the outcome shows deterioration on both sides.* Quality of mind and body suggests that observance of ethnic law is as great a necessity to a nation as immigration law." (Emphasis added.) Coolidge stated that "even though we need have no grave fears, now is the time for a careful reexamination and revision of our immigration policies."

The Spigot Gets Tighter— The 1921 Emergency Quota Law

As if on cue, about two months after Coolidge's essay appeared in *Good Housekeeping,* Congress voted on the proposed Emergency Quota Act of 1921, to adopt an immigration quota system for the first time in US history. Promoted as a temporary, fourteen-month emergency measure, the law, if passed, would cap the number of immigrants who could be admitted from any particular European country at 3 percent of the total number of foreign-born persons living in the United States from that country in 1910, according to the 1910 US census. It was a formula specifically designed to favor immigration from Northern and Western Europe and to limit immigration from Southern and Eastern Europe. This 3 percent plan was more liberal than a bill that had previously sailed through the House but been thwarted in the Senate, which would have suspended immigration altogether for two years.

On April 20, 1921, members of the House took to the floor to debate the 3 percent plan. Supporters decried the national immigration "crisis" and "great problem" of immigration requiring immediate action. They cited an unemployment rate that had risen to 5 percent, the vast numbers of non-English speakers in American cities, the bread lines in some cities, and the estimated 10 million immigrants living in the United States who had taken no steps to become citizens. They cited the rise of Bolshevist thought in Europe, and the concern that it was not the time to import into America the utter chaos of postwar Europe. As a matter of "first duty" to country, proclaimed Congressman Albert Johnson of Washington State (the bill's sponsor), immigration had to be strictly limited "until we have cleaned house here and know what we are going to do with the millions of unnaturalized aliens who are now here."

The oratory did not end there. Congressman Johnson and other proponents of the legislation also made perfectly clear their contempt for the "foreign element," informed by eugenic beliefs. As soon as he took to the House floor, Johnson entered into the record a letter he had procured from the State Department's leadership, which painted the worst possible caricature of would-be immigrants from Eastern Europe. Russian immigrants were described by the State Department as "highly undesirable as material for future American citizens. . . . The bulk of them have been habituated either to lawlessness or to the exercise of violence in the name of the law for so long that if not actually impregnated with bolshevism they are good material for Bolshevik propaganda." Polish immigrants (with a particular emphasis on Polish Jews) were described as "subnormal." The State Department warned that, even then, 35,000 Polish Jews were waiting in Warsaw for their American visas, writing:

> Six years of war and confusion and famine and pestilence
> have racked their bodies and twisted their mentality. . . . A

pitiably small percentage is moving with a fixed purpose. Hundreds, both Jewish and Christian, or those of no religious profession, have been asked why they wish to go America. The answer almost invariably is, "Please, mister, we have rich relatives there. We can find an easier life." These are not the Europeans of a sturdier day, who in family conference sternly resolved on the great adventure . . . to the new America across the seas. These are not those who hewed the forests, founded the towns, fought the savages, breasted the storms of wilderness, conquered the wastes, and built America. These are beaten folk, spirits broken, in effect driven from their European habitat into the west. They have no desire to form and build.

Congressman Lucian Walton Parrish of Texas took to the floor to echo those sentiments, regretting only that the proposed legislation did not go far enough. Parrish judged the flow of immigrants from Southern and Eastern Europe to be "one of the greatest emergencies that has ever confronted" the nation, proclaiming:

A study of the character of these immigrants discloses that many of them are restless, adventurous, and poverty stricken. Some of them have criminal habits and dispositions, and others are afflicted with the most terrible diseases known to the Old World, and to turn them loose into this country under the lax rules and regulations now in force is but to invite crime, dissension, disorder, and suffering. . . .

[N]ew and strange conditions have arisen in the countries over there; new and strange doctrines are being taught. . . . [T]here can be nothing so dangerous as for us to allow the undesirable foreign element to poison our civilization and thereby threaten the safety of the institutions that our fore-fathers have established for us.

Entirely absent from the majority's remarks was any acknowledgment of how immigrants from Southern and Eastern Europe were already thriving in America and had already contributed to society, including the great many who had just served in the US military during the First World War (including about 250,000 Jewish Americans).

So who spoke out on the House floor against the popular 3 percent quota plan—a bill that was sure to sail through Congress? Only a small contingent of mostly Jewish congressmen hailing from New York City. They spoke out, even though it subjected them to the accusation of having "dual loyalties" and caring more about Europeans than Americans. Mostly, I think they spoke up to go on record against arguments that were prejudice-inflected and fearmongering.

Albert Rossdale, a freshman congressman from New York (who will figure prominently in the Scheers' story to come—so I bid you to remember his name), took on Congressman Parrish of Texas, questioning whether Parrish's views stemmed from firsthand knowledge or were just a negative stereotype:

Mr. Chairman, the gentleman from Texas . . . assumes that all of these people over there are antagonistic to American ideals and interests. Has the gentleman ever come in contact with a lot of these immigrants and does he really know that they are of that type? I come from The Bronx, where there are a great many of these so-called foreigners, and I have an intimate knowledge of their political opinions and ideals, and I can say to the gentleman from Texas that if he had even a speaking acquaintance with them he would quickly learn that they breathe higher and purer ideals than he had any previous knowledge of. I invite the gentleman from Texas to come to The Bronx and find out for himself what splendid American citizens they make.

New York Representative Isaac Siegel argued that the only true crisis was Congress's severe underfunding of the recently created Department of Labor (established in 1913), which hampered the department from clearing the long backlogs of pending naturalization applications, funding Americanization programs, and stationing more doctors overseas to perform medical exams on would-be immigrants. "And I am very sorry," added Congressman Siegel, referring to the State Department letter entered into the record, "that we have people employed in the State Department who are imbued with certain perverted ideas so that they can send out stuff of that kind to be used in the Congress of the United States. . . . There is [no problem] except in the minds of the prejudiced, skilled agitator, who every year and every month is excited over the immigration question. It has become a part of his existence. He sees red everywhere he turns. It is his hobby in life."

Next spoke Representative William Bourke Cockran of New York, a famous orator of his day and a Tammany Hall Democrat. Cockran, of Irish descent, was a close friend of the Churchill family of England and even mentored the young Winston Churchill's oratorical skills. Cockran now employed wit in challenging the majority view:

Why, some gentlemen here spoke as though these immigrants were coming here for no other purpose than to blow up the Constitution, if they could get their hands on it. [Laughter.] Conceive for one moment the character of such a statement. That a man will come 5,000 or 6,000 miles, suffering the utmost hardships of a transatlantic voyage, parting with the last penny he owns in order to obtain passage, and all the time he is moved not by a desire to benefit himself but by a desire to blow up our Constitution! Now, think of that for a serious argument addressed to sensible men!

. . . We need the foreign laborer to make our soil fruitful, to make it fruitful of the basic raw materials on which skilled labor is exercised, without which, I venture to say, the great city of New York would not today be half its size. . . . The immigrant gives you the guaranty of love for our country by coming here. Surely the gentleman from Washington will not say for a moment that of the 10,000 that debark from vessels at our ports every week there is any considerable number who would want to blow up our Constitution, even if they could find out where it is located. [Laughter.]

Representative Meyer London, representing the Lower East Side added this:

Defenders of this bill thoughtlessly repeat the exploded theory that there have been two periods of immigration, the good period, which the chairman of the committee fixes up to the year 1900, and the bad period since. The strange thing about it is that at no time in history has any country made such rapid progress in industry, in science, and in the sphere of social legislation as this country has shown since 1900. The new immigration is neither different nor worse, and besides that, identically the same arguments were used against the old immigration. . . . Just now we hear nothing but hatred, nothing but the ravings of the exaggerated *I*—"I am of the best stock, I do not want to be contaminated; I have produced the greatest literature; my intellect is the biggest; my heart is the noblest"—and this is repeated in every parliament, in every country, by every fool all over the world.

The Emergency Quota Act of 1921 overwhelmingly passed both Houses of Congress and was signed by President Harding into law in May 1921. The vote in the Senate was ninety to two. No roll call was taken in the House. The Act represented a cataclysmic shift in US immigration policy, and it accomplished its purpose. Following its enactment, under the quota system, immigration to America plummeted by more than half—from 805,000 in 1921 to 309,000 in 1922. And the quotas sharply decreased immigration from Southern and Eastern Europe. The total number of Jewish immigrants dropped from 119,000 in 1921 to about 50,000 in 1922.

This much is clear: The Scheers were awfully lucky to have boarded the SS *Berengaria* when they did in 1922. Whether they knew it or not, they had managed to squeeze themselves into the last drops of the Great Jewish Migration—just as the spigot was being turned off. Had they waited eighteen months longer, they would have been stuck in Europe. That's because in 1924, Congress passed, and President Coolidge enthusiastically signed into law, even stricter quotas—the most restrictive immigration law in US history. By 1924, the spigot was shut. And the national origin quota system, devised to choke off undesirable immigration from Eastern and Southern Europe, essentially remained in place for the next forty years, until 1965.

The Scheers' Unheralded Angel on Their Journey to America: HIAS

Before we return to the Scheers' transatlantic voyage, and how they ended up in detention at Ellis Island, there is one more player to which you must be better introduced: HIAS.

Marion had always called Uncle Jake their "angel," and indeed he was—it was Jake who sponsored the Scheers to come to America and sent money for their passage. But how did Jake and Sarah even connect with each other during or after the war? How did Jake physically get money to Sarah and Meyer, in what was then Poland, to purchase the steamship tickets? How did Meyer, a Galician butcher who spoke not a word of English, navigate the US visa application process? There is another angel in this story besides Jake, and that angel is HIAS. (Originally named the Hebrew Sheltering and Immigrant Aid Society, its full name was later shortened to the Hebrew Immigrant Aid Society.) The Scheers' immigration story cannot be told without HIAS.

HIAS was created around the turn of the twentieth century in a storefront on the Lower East Side, when a group of Russian Jews who had settled in New York City gathered to bemoan some disturbing news: Jewish immigrants who died on Ellis Island were being buried in Potter's Field, without Jewish burial rites, because there was no one to do otherwise. They brainstormed about what they could do to help arriving Jewish immigrants. From those humble beginnings grew one of the most effective social service organizations of all time, which helped hundreds of thousands of Jewish immigrants and continues, to this day, to aid refugees from all over the world, regardless of religion.

Here is what HIAS did in the two decades leading up to the First World War: It successfully lobbied transatlantic ocean liners to improve conditions for all steerage passengers; in 1904, it established a bureau of Yiddish-speaking workers on Ellis Island to aid new arrivals and provide translation services; it successfully lobbied the US government to establish a kosher kitchen at Ellis Island, which opened in 1911; it provided legal services to help detainees challenge exclusion orders, establishing an office in Washington, DC; it ran a large shelter in New

York City that provided millions of meals and a roof over the heads of newly arrived Jewish immigrants; it helped thousands reach their final destinations after leaving Ellis Island, often providing the train fare needed to head west, north, and south. HIAS was also a hub for helping Jewish immigrants find employment; it sponsored night classes in English and "Americanization"; and it helped Jewish immigrants apply for US citizenship. By the time the First World War broke out, HIAS was a tour de force, headquartered in Manhattan with branch offices in multiple cities across in the United States.

Then, during the First World War, when immigration had largely ceased, HIAS stepped in to fill a different exigency—reconnecting frantic Jewish Americans with their scattered relatives in war-torn Europe. Even while the war raged, HIAS officers voyaged to Europe, opened an office in Rotterdam, and poured its energies into locating Jewish relatives in the German and Austro-Hungarian provinces, where most European Jews lived. Repeated petitions to the German and Austrian authorities finally resulted in HIAS being allowed by those enemy regimes to operate as a go-between. Thus, Jews in those territories could send short communications to HIAS, letting US relatives know their location and requesting financial assistance, and HIAS then delivered those communications and facilitated responses and the delivery of remittance funds. By the end of the war, HIAS's money transmitting function was so pronounced and effective that the New York State Banking Department insisted that HIAS register as a bank, which it did.

Thanks to HIAS, if Sarah Scheer had been able to communicate with Jake Green during the war, this was likely how. And it was likely through HIAS that Jake sent the Scheers money for passage to America.

But that is not all. When the First World War ended, and violence against Polish and Russian Jews accelerated, HIAS rushed in once again to carry out its mission of facilitating the legal immigration of Jews to America. Even as members of Congress were working to shut down Eastern European immigration, HIAS worked urgently in the opposite direction—using every legal tool at its disposal to assist European Jews in leaving Europe for as long as America's doors were still ajar. To that end, in 1920, HIAS established an office in Warsaw, Poland—the city where the US consulate was located—to smooth the immigration process. Working with Polish authorities, HIAS was able to reduce the waiting time for Polish Jews to obtain passports, from about six weeks to a few days; and working with American authorities in Warsaw, HIAS obtained consular approval for Jewish immigrants to fill out their visa applications in HIAS's Warsaw office—where a trained, Yiddish-speaking staff could help—before those immigrants had to appear at the US consulate for their visa interviews.

HIAS's work inured to the Scheers' benefit. When Meyer, Sarah, and their three children left Kopyczynce and traveled to Warsaw in 1922 to arrange for their papers to America, they followed a path paved in significant part by HIAS. Meyer almost certainly completed his family's visa application at HIAS's Warsaw office. And, as we shall see, HIAS was an angel to the Scheers on both sides of the Atlantic.

Time for Show and Tell: The Scheers' Entries in the Ship Manifest

Page 3351797, Lines 16 through 20 of the SS *Berengaria's* ship manifest. That may sound technical, but it's magical, because that is where the Scheers' transatlantic passage to America is recorded. Here, let's zoom in to see their names:

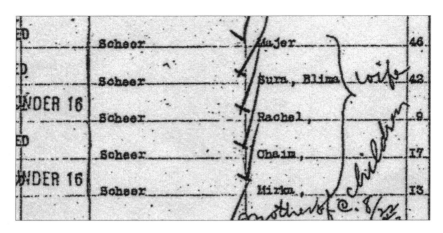

There they are: the Scheers: "Majer"—age 46, "Sura, Blima"—age 42, "Rachel"—age 9, "Chaim"—age 17, and "Mirka"—age 13. At Ellis Island, their manifest page and line number would become their quasi-"Social Security number." Immigrants were tracked throughout the inspection process using that information, which was often pinned to their coats.

The full pages of the ship manifest are too large to reprint here. Running across the top are more than twenty categories of questions, and running down each page—with one line per passenger—are the typed answers given by each passenger (or head of household). Questions about each passenger's age, sex, physical description, literacy, nationality, destination, occupation, health, financial condition, and so forth. All that information was recorded by the steamship companies and then promptly turned over to US immigration authorities when the ships docked in America.

None of this was done voluntarily, mind you. Congress, by law, had made steamship owners responsible for collecting the information needed to determine each passenger's eligibility for admission to the United States. The shipowners had excellent reason to comply with the law: their *pocketbooks*. Shipowners were charged a hefty penalty by the US government each time a passenger brought to American shores was deemed ineligible for admission by immigration authorities. A steerage ticket in 1922 cost about twenty-five dollars per passenger, but the steamship company could be fined as much as one hundred dollars for each passenger rejected at Ellis Island. On top of that, the steamship owner then had to transport the rejected passenger back to Europe and reimburse the US government for all meals provided to that passenger while detained at Ellis Island. Those costs added up. No wonder the shipping companies hired their own doctors to check the physical health of passengers, and screen the sick, before allowing them to board.

How Meyer Scheer Answered the Questions, As Recorded in the Ship Manifest

Let's look at how Meyer Scheer—speaking to the steamship officer at the port in Cherbourg, France—answered the questions put to him prior to boarding.

Physical Stuff

Meyer reported, and the ship doctor's examination confirmed, that all five Scheers were in "good" health. None were "deformed or crippled." They all had "fair" complexions, "dark" hair, and "dark" eyes.

Majer (Meyer) Scheer was listed as being five feet tall and as having the identifying mark of "favus gueri." *Favus* is a contagious fungal infection of the scalp. However, in Meyer's case, the ship doctor recorded that the favus was "gueri," which means "cured" in

French. So it would seem that Meyer had some visible scar on his scalp from an old, resolved infection.

Sura (Sarah) Blima was listed as being four feet, five inches—a typographical error. She was five feet, four inches, not four feet, five inches. Chaim (Hymie) was five feet, four inches. Mirka (Marion) was five feet, three inches (her fully grown adult height, again reflecting that she was no kindergartener when she immigrated.) Finally, Rachel (Ruthie) was listed as a "child," with no height measurement taken.

Race, Occupation, Destination

The manifest recorded the Scheers' nationality as "Galician" and their race as "Hebrew." Meyer, a "butcher"; Sarah, a "housewife." All five Scheers were listed as able to read and write in both "Jewish" and "Polish" (except for Ruthie, who could read and write only in "Jewish").

The Scheers' final destination was listed as New York, for the stated purpose of becoming US citizens. Meyer reported that his family was going to join his brother-in-law Jacob Green, who lived at "903 Tinton Avenue in New York City N.Y." He listed his cousin Elka in Kopyczynce as their "nearest relative" in Europe. Meyer also confirmed that he was neither a polygamist, nor an anarchist, nor had his family ever been supported by a charity.

Money

The trickiest question for Meyer was the one asking who had paid for his family's passage to America. That question was tricky for all steerage passengers. It was hardly uncommon for American relatives to assist with passage costs. But to avoid being labeled the dreaded

LPC (likely public charge), immigrants were incentivized to say they had paid their own way. And according to the ship manifest, that is what Meyer did. He told the ship officer in Cherbourg that he had paid for all five tickets himself.

The SS *Berengaria* Docks in New York Harbor

The SS *Berengaria* docked in Manhattan on September 20, 1922, with about 3,300 passengers on board. It arrived two days later than expected, and two days before the start of the Jewish New Year, Rosh Hashanah. The popular "Shipping News" section of the *New York Tribune* announced the ship's arrival in its morning edition.

And wouldn't you know it? . . . That same morning, the *New York Tribune* carried this front-page headline:

Harvard Asks Race and Color Of New Students

Revised Admission Blank Also Calls for Father's Birthplace and Whether Name Has Been Changed

Jews Consider It a Ban

University Authorities Insist No Race Is Aimed At; Seek Information

For the first time in Harvard's 286 years, incoming students would now be required to state their race and skin color in addition to religious preference. As the *Tribune* reported:

> These are radical and intimate questions and cause a considerable number of people to believe that the application blank is just another drive against the Jewish race, although the Harvard authorities through Professor Henry Pennypacker, chairman of the admission board, spiritedly maintained that such is not the case, and that the data that are sought are not so much a matter of record as they are of general interest.

How ironic that on the day my grandmother arrived in America, Harvard was narrowing the door on Jews, and that sixty-six years later, I would arrive in Cambridge as a Harvard freshman and live in *Pennypacker Hall*. Like I said before, this country is both magnificent and complex.

My Theory as to How Meyer's Heart Murmur Came to Be Detected at Ellis Island

The Great Hall at Ellis Island was an exceptionally loud place. To be sure, loads of doctors with the national Public Health Service performed visual examinations of incoming immigrants as they walked through the Great Hall. But it was simply too loud to listen to anyone's heart. So how did Ellis Island officials come to detect Meyer's heart murmur?

Here is my theory. Meyer was in line with Hymie. Meyer may have looked thin and pale, but healthy looking enough to pass the visual inspections. But when he got to the US immigration inspector, who stood peering at the ship manifest, the inspector saw the notation of a scar on Meyer's scalp—that "favus gueri" mark of identification from a past infection. My theory is that the simple notation of this past infection in the manifest was enough to trigger the Ellis Island inspector to send Meyer for a further medical exam. And it was there, in the quiet of an Ellis Island medical examination room, that Meyer's heart murmur was heard for the first time in his forty-six-year life.

However the murmur came to be detected, after its discovery, Inspector Bishara (whose first name is not stated in the file) wasted no time. He promptly declared Meyer and the entire Scheer family ineligible for entry into the United States. Bishara handwrote onto the ship manifest, *Page 3351797, Line 16,* that Meyer Scheer had been certified to have "valvular disease of [the] heart":

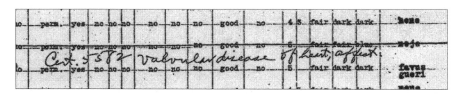

Bishara ordered the entire Scheer family excluded, to be returned to Europe. And with that, the Scheers' struggle to stay in the United States had begun.

☎

A Telephone Call: August 1992

Lisa:	Good morning, Grandma.
Marion:	Lisa?
Lisa:	Yes, yes, it's me. How are you feeling today?
Marion:	Not good, darling. Between the leg and the eye and the pinched nerve, I'm on my way out.
Lisa:	I'm sorry to hear that.
Marion:	And it's worse than a cemetery here. You don't see anyone come and go. But look, you get old, so what can you expect? You gotta face the music. It's just too bad, because I wanted to be to your wedding.
Lisa:	Forget about my wedding, Grandma. Your grandson is getting married next week!
Marion:	Yeah, I'll give him a nice gift. What, you think I won't give any money when my grandson gets married even if he never picks up the phone, though he knows I am all alone?
Lisa:	Well, Grandma, he must be busy.
Marion:	So, tell me something new. Are you meeting any nice fellows?
Lisa:	I'm dating one guy right now.
Marion:	Is he Jewish?
Lisa:	No.
Marion:	Okay, so you'll go out and have a good time. Order the nicest dinner. You see, you don't have to be religious—I don't care if you mix your dishes, but you should marry someone Jewish. This gentile will *shlep* [drag] you off to Europe.

82

CHAPTER THREE

Thirty-Three Days and Nights at Ellis Island

We Were Pulling Our Hair Out

G O BACK TO EUROPE, THEY ORDERED us. To Europe! To that black hole. My father sent a telegram to Uncle Jake, and the next day, Jake, Louis, and Aunt Annie came to see us in detention. Mama and her brothers wept and hugged. It was the first time seeing one another in more than thirty years. My uncles wore fine coats and looked worried. Aunt Annie kissed us and smiled and spoke to me and Ruthie a few words in Jewish. But this was not a time for getting to know one another. The adults needed to talk about how to stop the inspectors from sending us back to Europe on the next boat.

And so we waited at Ellis Island. Day after day we waited on that island—my father and Hymie in the men's ward, and Ruthie and me with Mama in the women's ward. It was terrifying, the waiting, especially since we couldn't even see our father. I even missed Hymie's teasing. Yom Kippur came and went. In our women's ward,

I watched Mama and the other Jewish women daven the *Kol Nidre*, tears streaming down their cheeks.

The dormitories were crowded, full with people ordered sent back or waiting for hearings. There were rows of bunk beds, except they looked more like hammocks hanging on metal chains, three stacked one on top of the other. Every afternoon they let us into a locked courtyard to take in fresh air and move around, and every third day we took showers. Some of the girls I met there had a parent sick in the Ellis Island hospital, on the other side of the island. The worst kind of diagnosis was tuberculosis or trachoma—if someone had a contagious disease, they were almost definitely being sent back.

And yet, even in detention, even on that windy island, there was life. Desperation, yes, but also life. At 6:00 every morning, the "matron" woke us all up and asked Mama's permission for Ruthie and me to go with the other children to classes for learning a few words of English or sewing. Mama always said yes. Ruthie and I sat on a bench with the other children and learned. They gave us milk and graham crackers.

They even had a kosher kitchen on Ellis Island. I remember one day they gave me a banana to eat—but *who knew from a banana in Galicia?* I had never seen one and had no idea what to do with that yellow thing. So I traded the banana with another girl for something else.

Mama was anxious all the time. From our dormitory bathroom, we looked at the Statue of Liberty, which seemed like a cruel trick. Here we were so close to it, but locked up.

Aunt Annie, Our Savior

And then, *finally*, they let us in.

You want to know how it happened? I'll tell you. Aunt Annie, God bless her, was our savior. She took the train to Washington, to the Capitol. And there she spoke to President Coolidge. Aunt Annie was American born, you see, and she knew these things and spoke a perfect English. She convinced President Coolidge to let us come in. My Uncle Jake had to pay over a lot of money—God bless him too, such a good man—and they let us in. Finally, we left Ellis Island and went with Uncle Jake to the Bronx. Never were we so happy in all our lives!

ENTER: THE HISTORY DETECTIVE

Taking on the Legend

So that's it—that is the legend I heard growing up of how the Scheers managed to stay in America, of how Aunt Annie had saved them by personally speaking with President Coolidge.

Oh, I do so love the image of Aunt Annie, wife of a cloakmaker, herself a first-generation Bronx daughter of Galician immigrants, boarding a locomotive to meet with President Coolidge in Washington. But it is a myth. So too is a second version of the legend (passed down to Ruthie's daughter) in which Aunt Annie saved the family by allegedly petitioning Franklin Roosevelt. (As a historical footnote, Roosevelt had entirely withdrawn from public life in 1922 to deal with his polio diagnosis, and Coolidge was still the vice president in the fall of 1922.) This is not to say that Aunt Annie played no role in rescuing the Scheers; she did. But the historical records that I've unearthed tell a different story of how things happened.

Before I tell you what I found, allow me to share *how* I found it out. Like a great treasure map, no step was wasted on this journey. When Ellis Island held no answers for me, I was pointed to the US Department of Labor, which was in charge of immigration enforcement in the 1920s. The department no longer held any records for me (it had long since been divested of authority over immigration matters), but it led me to the US Department of Homeland Security, my next stop. My big break came in 2015, when the chief of the Genealogy Section for the US Citizenship and Immigration Services (USCIS), part of Homeland Security, responded to my inquiry by advising that the Scheers' immigration file had been part of a series transferred decades earlier to the National Archives in Washington, DC. As if to discourage me from getting my hopes up, he wrote: "The file may or may not relate to your immigrant and may or may not have survived." I had only one place left to go. I wrote to the National Archives.

And then it came in the mail. A big, fat envelope from the National Archives, enclosing a copy of the Scheers' immigration file. The archivists had located it, sitting on the proverbial (and perhaps literal) dusty shelf, undisturbed, these nearly hundred years. Eureka!

The narrative I will now share—faithfully based on those excavated records—is all at once a human drama, political drama, and mystery. Human drama—because this story is replete with emergency telegrams, gut-wrenching choices, love, separation, despair, and even testimony from a long-lost brother. Political drama—because it reveals that the Scheers were ultimately saved by New York politicians. For me, who grew up harboring a certain skepticism of politics (a skepticism reinforced by the professional years I spent investigating and prosecuting public corruption), what a shocker it was to learn that my family owes its life in America to the intervention of politicians, Republican and Democrat. It has caused me to rethink politics and value more dearly the service that good politicians can provide.

And, finally, this story is part mystery because I am still not sure of the *why*. I can tell you what happened, and when and where it happened, but I cannot tell you definitively why it happened; that is, why multiple elected politicians—three New York congressmen and one New York US senator, to be precise—interceded to turn the fate of a small-town Galician butcher and his pencil-skinny wife and three kids. We'll tackle the why too.

Oh, and yes, there *was* a train ride from New York to Washington to save the Scheers. But it was not Aunt Annie on that train. The man who took that fateful ride was Walter Prendergast, a complete stranger to the Scheers, a thirty-three-year-old Irish American from Brooklyn, who was later described by the *New York Times* as "a chunky bulldog of a man, with steely blue eyes." Have I piqued your interest? Without further delay, let's dive into what happened.

How Politicians Saved the Scheers
September 22, 1922: Put in Detention

It is Friday, September 22, 1922, and Meyer Scheer is in a state of shock. Having finally made it to Ellis Island after his transatlantic journey, Meyer has now failed medical inspection and been ordered back to Europe with his family. All in one day, and on erev Rosh Hashanah, no less. The inspector has declared Meyer "physically defective" and thus ineligible to enter America on account of a heart murmur he never knew he had. Furthermore, because Meyer is the head of his household, the entire family has been declared "likely public charges," and thus likewise deemed ineligible to enter. The Scheers are led from the Great Hall of Ellis Island to the dormitories, where they will stay until the next ship can take them back to Europe. They are far from alone; they are part of the spike in deportations ordered in 1922 as Ellis Island inspectors exercise their broad authority to keep people out, consistent with the law and restrictionist mood of the nation.

Meyer, who speaks no English, manages to get a telegram to Uncle Jake, sharing the disastrous news. There is a Western Union office on the second floor of Ellis Island for circumstances like this. Meanwhile, Ellis Island clerks dutifully begin counting the meals eaten by the Scheers while in detention. Each "breakfast," "dinner," and "supper" is neatly recorded in the official records so that the US authorities can charge those meal costs back to the shipping carrier, as a penalty for having brought these defective aliens to American shores.

September 23, 1922: The Scheers Fight Exclusion

Day 2 of Detention. The Scheers file a legal petition challenging their exclusion order. This is HIAS's doing. HIAS maintains an office on the premises at Ellis Island, staffed with Yiddish-speaking representatives who provide legal and social services to Jewish detainees. The fact that this urgent legal filing occurs on a Saturday (the Sabbath) and on the holy day of Rosh Hashanah is of no moment. The Scheers' petition asks for a hearing to challenge the finding that they are likely to become public charges. Ellis Island personnel record the filing—look at the third line from the bottom of the image on the next page—indicating that "Majer Scheer wf & chldn" are among the fourteen habeas corpus petitions filed that day.

Judging by the other names on this list (Aristides Jaimedes, Vincenzo Esposito, Abigail Naranjo De Villamizar), the Scheers are in detention with immigrants from Greece, Italy, Spain, and elsewhere.

```
Habeas Corpus                    Ellis Island            9/23/22ww

55,151-82    Mousa Hatela
55,151-83    Ishmail Shehadeh
55,151-84    Seva Solomon
55,265-144   Volce,Riva,Calman,Haim,Zalman,Leib & Ruchla
             Samis
55,265-21    Vincenzo Esposito
55,265-273   Olimpia Ravano
55,265-136   Maria,Rosario Galla
55,145-40    Aristides Jaimedes wf Georgia
55,265-390   Fruma Wilensky & dau.
55,265-461   Anna Gnersin
55,265-811   Anna & Stanislaw Stuchlik
55,265-741   Majer Scheer wf & chldn
55,265-442   Basha Kuchardski
55,210-154   Abigail Naranjo De Villamizar
```

While awaiting their hearing, Meyer and Hymie live in the men's ward, Sarah and the girls in the women's ward. During such busy, congested times at Ellis Island, the separation of the sexes is strictly enforced.

September 26, 1922: Testimony at Ellis Island

Day 5 of Detention. Today is the legal hearing for which Meyer petitioned. The wait hasn't been long. Testimony will be taken on Ellis Island before the Board of Special Inquiry, a three-man immigration panel composed of Ellis Island inspectors who will decide the Scheers' challenge to the exclusion order.

Meyer Scheer is ushered into the hearing room, which looks like a small courtroom. It has two tall windows and is all wood and metal. At the front, on a raised platform, sits a long, heavy wooden table, outfitted with brass, goose-necked lamps, and four chairs. Those are the chairs for the three board members—Connor, Travis, and Scarlett are their names—and for the official stenographer. Two metal fans, affixed to the walls, are whirring. It is a hot September. A wooden bar that runs the length of the room physically separates the board members from where the immigrant and his or her witnesses will stand and testify. Wooden benches and chairs, seating for at least twenty people, occupy the small gallery. Perhaps unsurprisingly, the room feels light and airy, save for the heavy wooden furniture, because sunlight streams in through the windows, bouncing off New York Harbor. This is an island, after all.

Meyer is the only member of his immediate family present. Gratefully, he is accompanied by the three supporting witnesses who arrived that morning on the nine A.M. Ellis Island ferry from Battery Park. His witnesses are Jake Green (Sarah's brother), Annie Green (the wife of Sarah's other brother, Louis Green), and a third person, Joseph Scheer, Meyer's biological brother. (Wait . . . who is this Joseph Scheer? Until I found his testimony in the immigration file, it had been totally lost to family memory that Meyer Scheer had any siblings living in New York in 1922.) A Yiddish interpreter named Driller is also present. There is no indication of any attorney for the Scheers being present. And if a HIAS representative is present, the stenographer fails to note it.

The board is eager to get on with it and calls the hearing to order. There is no time to waste. Ellis Island has a shortage of bed space and this board has more than a dozen hearings to preside over today.

The hearing kicks off with the board documenting why the Scheer family was ordered excluded: namely, four days earlier, Inspector Bishara determined Meyer Scheer to be "PH. DEF. LPC"—an alien with a physical defect (PH. DEF.) who would likely become a public charge (LPC) of the state if admitted. The board cites the medical certificate issued by an Ellis Island doctor, who certifies that Meyer Scheer is "afflicted with Valvular disease of the heart, which may affect ability to earn a living."

Meyer's Testimony

Meyer is the first witness up. Never before in his life has he testified at a legal proceeding. Testifying through a Yiddish interpreter, Meyer must be terribly nervous. Chairman Connor swears him in.

Meyer responds to a litany of questions as the stenographer takes it all down on a Remington typewriter. Click-clack, click-clack, the sound of the typewriter keys filling every pause. Yes, my son and I are butchers. My wife is a housewife. My daughters are schoolchildren. Who paid our passage? "My wife's two brothers in the US, Jacob and Louis Green, paid passage." Meyer admits this now, contradicting his earlier representation in Cherbourg that he himself had paid the family's passage. I "have $230," Meyer says. "We are going to my wife's brother, Jacob Green, to remain permanently." Click-clack, click-clack.

Meyer then shows the inspectors the family's passports and the stenographer notes for the record that all five passports were "issued at Kopyczynce on August 10, 1922" and that the Scheers' visas were issued "by the American Consul at Warsaw Aug[ust] 26, 1922."

Do you have any relatives abroad? the board asks him. No, Meyer says (electing not to mention Cousin Elka in this moment). Still more questions:

Q. Have you any other children?

A. No.

Q. Have you any relatives in the United States?

A. I have two brothers and a sister of my own, Hersh, Josef and Sprince Farber, all living in New York City.

Q. How long have they been in the United States?

A. From 11 to 30 years.

91

Q. How long have you been following your occupation as [a] butcher?

A. Since childhood.

Q. How late were you working prior to embarkation?

A. We left on Sunday for the United States and on Thursday previous to that I worked.

Q. Have you required the services of a physician in recent years?

A. No.

Q. How do you expect to support yourself and family in the United States?

A. Work as butcher.

Uncle Jake's Testimony

Next up is Uncle Jake, who testifies in English:

Q. What is your name and where do you reside?

A. Jacob Green, 903 Tinton Avenue, Bronx, New York.

Q. For whom do you call?

A. My sister, her husband and their three children (names them).

Q. Are you a citizen?

A. Yes (shows certificate of naturalization 1419503 issued in the Supreme Court, Bronx County, New York, May 27, 1920).

Q. Are you married?

A. Yes, I have a wife and 4 children; the eldest child is 23 years; the others are 20, 18, and 10 years of age.

Q. What is your business?

A. I am in the cloak and suit business in partnership with one by the name of Pollak. I have personally invested about $10,000 in the business and draw $80 a week.

Q. Have you a personal bank account?

A. No, but I have a business account in the Chatham and Phenix Bank in which there is [a] $24,000 balance.

Q. Have you the book with you or a statement from the bank to that effect?

A. No.

Q. Why do you carry such a large balance in the bank?

A. It is a business account.

Q. Have you any property?

A. No.

Q. With whom are your sister, her husband and their family to live?

A. With me; I have six rooms.

Q. Has your sister any other relatives in the United States?

A. Yes.

Q. Did you contribute towards the passage of these people?

A. Yes.

Q. Majer Scheer has been certified as having valvular disease of the heart. Knowing this, what are you willing to do for him?

A. I will do everything that is to be done for him.

Q. There is no doubt he will require medical treatment and will you pay for that and see that they do not become public charges?

A. Yes.

Q. Will you see that the children go to school till they are 16 years of age?

A. Yes.

Notice how Uncle Jake, by all accounts a successful businessman, possesses no personal bank account and owns no house. As for his business account at the Chatham and Phenix (one of the country's ten largest banks at the time), the board suspiciously questions why on earth anyone would keep $24,000 ("such a large balance") in the bank. Times were different. Perhaps the board is prescient, because when the stock market crashes seven years later, in 1929, banks freeze people's money and approximately 9,000 banks fail. Luckily for Jake, the Chatham and Phenix does not fail. It merges at some point with Manufacturers Trust, which later becomes Chase Bank.

Aunt Annie's Testimony

Next, Aunt Annie testifies. Naturally, with her "perfect English" (as Marion described it), Annie testifies in English:

Q. What is your name and where do you reside?

A. Anna Green; my husband's name is Louis Green; I reside at 1941 Fowler Avenue, Bronx, New York.

Q. For whom do you call?

A. The Scheer family; she is my husband's sister.

Q. How long is your husband in the United States?

A. 27 years; he is a citizen; his papers are at home.

Q. How many children have you?

A. Two children; 15 & 17 years of age.

Q. What is your husband's business or occupation?

A. Cloak and suit business for himself; he has about $12,000 invested and draws $60 a week.

Q. Have you or your husband money in the bank?

A. I have $700 in the Cosmopolitan Bank.

Q. Do you or your husband own any property?

A. Yes, a house worth $10,000 on which there is a $3,500 mortgage.

Q. What interest have you in your brother-in-law and his family?

A. I am willing to assist in their care and maintenance.

So we know from this testimony that, by September 1922, Louis and Anna Green have become homeowners—probably my first American relatives to own property.

Joseph Scheer's Testimony

Finally, Meyer's biological brother, Joseph Scheer, is called. He testifies through the Yiddish interpreter:

Q. What is your name and where do you reside?

A. Joseph Scheer, 294 East 3rd Street, New York City.

Q. For whom do you call?

A. My brother and his family.

Q. How long are you in this country?

A. Since 1907.

Q. Have you declared your intention of becoming a citizen?

A. No.

Q. Are you married?

95

A. Yes, I have a wife and 7 children; the eldest is 18 years and the youngest 5 years.

Q. What is your business or occupation?

A. Furrier, earning $75 a week.

Q. Have you money in the bank?

A. I have $400 in the Bowery Bank; the book is at home.

Q. Do you own property?

A. No.

Q. What are you willing to do for your brother and his family?

A. Assist in their care and maintenance.

Q. What is your brother's occupation?

A. Butcher.

Q. Does he sell meat or kill cattle?

A. He sells meat.

Joseph Scheer's progress in America has apparently been slower than that of Jake and Louis Green. Fifteen years after immigrating to America, Joseph still lives and works on the Lower East Side as a garment industry worker. He has not yet applied for US citizenship and testifies in Yiddish, suggesting he may not be fluent in English. But he says he has money in the bank and is willing to help support his brother Meyer's family.

It is now decision time for the board. The hearing seems to have gone well, right? After all, three witnesses have personally testified to their willingness to financially support the Scheers, and two of those witnesses have solid financial assets. Moreover, Meyer, despite his recent and surprising cardiac diagnosis, has been gainfully working all these years as a butcher, unimpaired. Nevertheless, it takes just a moment for the board to reject the Scheers' petition:

Inspector Travis:	I move that the alien Majer Scheer be excluded as a person suffering with a physical defect which may affect his ability to earn a living, and that all be excluded as persons likely to become public charges and as assisted aliens.
Inspector Scarlett:	I second the motion.
Chairman:	I make it unanimous.

The exclusion order stands. Not only that, but in denying the Scheers' petition, the Board of Special Inquiry expands the justification for exclusion, additionally deeming the Scheers to be "assisted aliens" because their transatlantic passage was paid for by someone other than themselves. Meyer's admission of this fact has cost him. The Scheers' exclusion order now stands as firmly as a three-legged stool: Meyer is "physically defective"; the family members are "likely public charges"; and they are "assisted aliens" to boot.

The board notifies Meyer of his right to appeal to the secretary of labor in Washington, whose decision is final.

> Q. Do you wish to appeal?
>
> A. Yes.

Meyer is further told that, if he is deported, the secretary of labor may "in his discretion" order a refund of the Scheers' passage money.

> Q. In that event, to whom do you wish it sent?
>
> A. To myself, Majer Scheer, in care of the Postmaster at Kopyczynce, Eastern Galicia, Poland.

The final words on the hearing transcript page read: "EXCLUDED AND ORDERED DEPORTED." Look at how Meyer—standing in that hearing room, signs his last name to the appeal, with a shaky hand:

Date *Sept 26, 1922*,

To the

Honorable Secretary of Labor

(Through official channels):

I desire to appeal from the decision

of the Board of Special Inquiry.

Moyer Scher
(Name.)

"Scher." Only one "e." Perhaps he doesn't know how to spell his name in English. Or perhaps, in this fraught moment, Aunt Annie leans over Meyer's shoulder and whispers to him that "Scher" sounds more American. Because from this moment on—regardless of how the immigration authorities spell the Scheers' surname in official paperwork—they call themselves the Scher family.

September 27, 1922: HIAS at Work

Day 6 of Detention. One day after the unsuccessful hearing at Ellis Island, HIAS shoots an urgent telegram to Uncle Jake. "PLEASE SEE US RE MEYER SHEER [sic] FAMILY VERY URGENT. HIAS ELLIS ISLAND." HIAS is preparing the appeal to the Department of Labor. Meanwhile, the HIAS representative jots this in the file: "Albert B. Rossdale, 87 Chambers St." Someone has reached out to Congressman Albert Rossdale about the Scheers' case.

October 1, 1922: Yom Kippur on Ellis Island

Day 10 of Detention. It is the holiest night of the Jewish calendar—erev Yom Kippur. Meyer and Hymie gather in the men's ward with other Jewish male detainees. HIAS has ferried a rabbi over to Ellis Island to chant the Kol Nidre. What words might Meyer have offered to his son, or Sarah to her daughters, on this holiest of holy days, when they are without liberty and without country? Hopefully, prayer is a comfort to them.

October 4, 1922: The Case Goes to Washington

Day 13 of Detention. Ellis Island officials want the Scheers gone—five beds to be freed up—so they write to headquarters, asking that Meyer's appeal be expedited in time for the next ship back to Europe. "The [medical] certificate against the head of the family is the controlling feature of the case. EXPEDITE DECISION; next sailing Oct. 13th," they write.

October 7, 1922: Politicians Go on Record—Congressmen Albert Rossdale and Nathan Perlman and Power Broker Simon Wolf

Day 16 of Detention. Expedited review has been granted and today the Scheers' appeal comes before the Department of Labor's Board of Review in Washington. This board of review is a body of recent vintage. Secretary of Labor James Davis created it in January 1922 to help address the crushing number of appeals from deportation and exclusion orders, all of which must be finally decided by his office. The board is nothing if not efficient. It arranges for prompt hearings of counsel or relatives of detained parties, delivers same-day recommendations to the secretary's office, and thus assures that immigration appeals can be heard, considered, and finally decided all in the same day. As Secretary Davis later reports to President Coolidge in his 1923 annual report, the board of review "has proved a most valuable adjunct to the Secretary's Office."

Meyer is not present at this appeals hearing. He and his family are in detention back on Ellis Island. But the presence of an "Attorney Gottlieb" is noted as appearing on the Scheers' behalf. Once again, this is HIAS. Attorney Gottlieb is Louis S. Gottlieb, the head of HIAS's legal office in Washington. The stenographer also notes for the record: "Congressman Perlman interested."

There is no transcript of what Gottlieb says to the board of review, but he evidently fails to persuade. The board's chairman, A. E. Reitzel, perfunctorily recommends that the Ellis Island exclusion order be affirmed:

> These Polish Hebrew aliens were excluded as lpc and assisted, and the man in addition as physically defective, he being certified for valvular disease of the heart. He is a butcher by trade. Aliens were destined to two brothers and a sister of the man in this country. The relatives are comparatively well-to-do. However, inasmuch as the defect against the man is of a serious nature and as it affects his ability to earn a living, it is believed that exclusion should occur.

Later that same day, Robe Carl White, the second assistant secretary of the Department of Labor, adopts and "so orders" the recommendation.

Robe Carl White is a lawyer from Indiana, now in charge of all immigration matters for the Department of Labor. It is White's third month in this important government post, having been named to it in July 1922. Because of the rise in immigration appeals, Secretary Davis told President Harding and Congress that he could not manage with just one assistant secretary of labor, so Congress funded the position of a second assistant secretary of labor over immigration, and President Harding gave White the job. Effectively, Robe Carl White is the final decider of all immigration appeals for the Department of Labor.

But what's this? . . . on the bottom of White's affirmation order, someone handwrites in pencil: Congressman Perlman and Simon Wolf both "advised this date October 7, 1922," and Congressman Rossdale "advised this date October 9, 1922."

Who are these three men—Rossdale, Perlman, and Wolf? Let's meet them before we continue with our story.

Albert Rossdale. 1921. Library of Congress. Harris & Ewing Photograph

This is Representative Albert Berger Rossdale. A New York City native, Rossdale worked as a post office clerk and in a jewelry business before successfully running for Congress in 1920. He represents the Twenty-Third District, composed of parts of the Bronx, and thus I believe he is the Greens' local congressman. Jake or Louis or Annie Green must have reached out to him. Rossdale is Republican, Jewish, and pro-immigration. He is the upstart congressman who, the year before, in 1921, energetically spoke out during the House floor debate on the Emergency Quota Act. When Congressman Lucian Walton Parrish of Texas characterized Eastern Europeans as an "undesirable foreign element," it was Rossdale who had invited "the gentleman from Texas to come to The Bronx and find out for himself what splendid American citizens they make." Rossdale is up for reelection on November 7, 1922—just one month away—running for a second term in Congress.

Nathan Perlman. 1920. Library of Congress.
National Photo Company Collection

This is Nathan Perlman. When he enters our story in October 1922, Perlman is a second-term Republican congressman representing New York's Fourteenth Congressional District, then composed of parts of Manhattan. Born in Poland, Perlman is also Jewish and came to the United States at the age of three, later becoming a naturalized US citizen. After graduating from the College of the City of New York and New York University Law School, he entered public life and was first elected to Congress in 1918. Perlman is also up for reelection on November 7, 1922—running for his third term.

Simon Wolf. Date unknown. Courtesy Capital Jewish Museum

This is Simon Wolf. When Simon Wolf enters our story in October 1922, he is already an old man—eighty-five years old. Wolf is not an elected official, but a Washington power broker, considered to be one of the most influential Jewish American advocates of the day. As one historian recounts: Wolf was the "political confidant of every Republican president from Abraham Lincoln to Taft."

Born in Bavaria, Wolf immigrated to America in 1848 as part of that wave of German Jewish immigration in the mid-1800s. After originally settling in Ohio, Wolf moved to Washington, DC, where he spent decades practicing law and participating in political life. He was named DC's recorder of deeds, and later the US consul to Egypt. Wolf also led numerous Jewish American organizations: The Union of American Hebrew Congregations, the Order of B'nai Brith, and, important for our story, from 1911 through 1914, Wolf was a lawyer for HIAS and personally handled Washington legal appeals on behalf of Jewish detainees. In 1913, after HIAS opened a permanent office in Washington (run by Louis Gottlieb), Wolf continued to provide counsel to HIAS as needed.

Simon Wolf was so dedicated throughout his life to dispelling prejudice and misinformation about Jewish Americans that, in 1891, when a popular magazine claimed that Jewish Americans tended to evade military service, Wolf spent over three years at his own cost and effort compiling the names of every Jewish soldier who had fought in American wars, from the American Revolution to the War of 1812 to the Mexican-American War to the Civil War. In 1895, he published all those names and the stories behind the soldiers in *The American Jew as Patriot, Soldier and Citizen.* When the tide of US policy began to turn against immigration in the early 1900s, Wolf took up the cause of keeping the spigot open for Jewish immigration as best he could—by, among other things, testifying before Congress that Jews should not be singled out as a "race" by immigration officials.

Wolf, like Congressmen Rossdale and Perlman, lent his respected name to the Scheers' case.

Now that we've met Congressmen Rossdale and Perlman, and Simon Wolf, let's return to the Scheers' struggle to stay in America.

October 9, 1922: Efforts by the Greens

Day 18 of Detention. The Greens (Jake, Louis, and Annie) are frantically trying to figure out what more they can do to keep the Scheers from being sent back to Europe. They enlist the help of Dr. Hyman Goldstein, a respected Lexington Avenue physician, who writes to HIAS on October 9, asking whether it would be possible for him to reexamine Meyer on Ellis Island "in the presence of the resident physician." HIAS relays back that, unfortunately, "the policy of the authorities . . . is not to permit any "outside physician [to be] present at such reexamination."

October 10, 1922: The Scheers' Case Is Reconsidered

Day 19 of Detention. The Scheers' exclusion order has already been upheld twice, first by the Board of Special Inquiry at Ellis Island, and then by the Department of Labor Board of Review in Washington. What happens now? Congressman Rossdale presses the Department of Labor to reconsider the Scheers' appeal again. The request is granted. On October 10, Congressman Rossdale dispatches his personal secretary to attend the hearing in Washington to advocate for the Scheers' admission.

"This case comes before the Board of Review for reconsideration. Secretary to Congressman Rossdale heard."

There is no transcript of what the congressman's secretary says to the board, but he too fails to persuade. The board doesn't budge. Its recommendation:

These aliens, natives of Poland, arrived at Ellis Island September 22, 1922. They were all excluded as likely to become public charges and as assisted aliens, and in addition thereto the husband and father as physically defective (valvular disease of the heart). Under date of October 7 the Department affirmed the excluding decision.

New York recommends exclusion.

In view of the fact that the head of the family is certified for a physical defect which may affect his ability to earn a living the Board of Review recommends that the former excluding decision be permitted to stand.

That recommendation is adopted the same afternoon. The exclusion order stands, yet again.

The situation is now dire for the Scheers. Top brass at the Department of Labor have repeatedly affirmed the exclusion order and *in only three days,* on October 13, the ship back to Europe will depart from New York Harbor.

A last-ditch attempt is made to stall. Attorney Louis Gottlieb of HIAS files an emergency petition that same afternoon in federal court in Manhattan, challenging the exclusion order again. It's a Hail Mary move because the exclusion order against the Scheers is not lawless. To the contrary, it is law*ful.* It is fully in keeping with the letter and spirit of the immigration laws in place in 1922, which give immigration officials broad authority to keep out those deemed medically unfit. And the order has been upheld repeatedly after giving the Scheers due process at multiple hearings. Gottlieb surely knows this; Congressman Rossdale knows this; and the Scheers must know this if they are being candidly counseled.

And yet, the stall tactic works. Before the day is out, Ellis Island notifies immigration headquarters in Washington: We "have been served with a writ of habeas corpus" in the case of Majer Scheer and wife and children who arrived on the *Berengaria,* and "shall promptly notify you of the proceedings thereon." While this legal process remains pending, Ellis Island officials suspend their plans to put the Scheers on that October 13 ship back to Europe.

October 12, 1922: A Gut-Wrenching Proposal

Day 21 of Detention. The Scheers' stall tactic cannot work for long. Time is running out and options must be weighed. Impossibly hard options.

Congressman Rossdale's office requests yet another reconsideration hearing before the board of review—this time to make a proposal. The request is granted. On October 12, Congressman Rossdale's secretary returns once more to address the board in Washington. The proposal is a gut-wrenching one:

"Request is now made that the children be admitted."

Click-clack, click-clack, the stenographer types out those nine words. But consider their import. "Request is now made that the children be admitted," meaning: Let the children stay and the parents will return to Europe.

The unthinkable has become thinkable. The proposal is for Meyer and Sarah to accept the exclusion order for themselves and return to Europe on that October 13 ship, without their children, if only their three children can stay in the United States. Knowing this means they will likely never see their children again, Meyer and Sarah make this proposal. Meyer and Sarah, who lost seven of their children in infancy, are now willing to let go of the three who lived, if only Hymie, Mirka, and Ruchel can stay in America.

How has this proposal come to be made, I wonder. Is it based on HIAS's experienced advice that the Scheers were now truly at their rope's end? Is it Uncle Jake or Aunt Annie's idea? Or perhaps Rossdale's? I picture Annie ferrying over to Ellis Island to obtain Meyer's urgent authorization. *We'll adopt the children as our own and take care of them, Meyer. There is no alternative, except all of you going back.* The physical barrier between Meyer and Sarah, locked in separate wards, must be crushing at this moment. Meyer and Sarah cannot meet or hug. If they communicate at all about the proposal, it is likely through a HIAS volunteer shuttling messages between the wards. Is Sarah even told of the proposal in advance? Maybe Meyer keeps it from her—knowing the news will break her fragile frame once and for all. Or maybe Sarah is told and gives her immediate blessing, with the strength of a mother who will sacrifice anything for the sake of her children. The historical record provides no answers to these questions other than to confirm that this gut-wrenching proposal is made. The children are not told.

Thank goodness in retrospect, the proposal is swiftly denied. Here is the board's recommendation:

> In view of the fact that the family seems to be coming here as a unit, the Board of Review recommends that the former excluding decision be permitted to stand.

So ordered by Robe Carl White. A handwritten note at the bottom of the document reads: "Cong. Rossdale advised this date, 10-13-22."

October 14, 1922: Enter an Even Bigger Gun— Senator William Musgrave Calder

Day 23 of Detention. HIAS telegrams Uncle Jake the bad news: "REGRET ADVISE WASHINGTON ORDERES [*SIC*] DEPORTATION OF SCHEER FAMILY. HIAS ELLIS ISLAND." There is a palpable note of defeat. The telegram suggests no further course of action. The Scheers' fight to enter America looks hopeless now.

Yet, in this moment of despair, something miraculous happens. An even bigger political gun intercedes to help the Scheers—the Republican US senator from New York, William Musgrave Calder. I believe this is Congressman Rossdale's doing (though I have no documentation to prove it). After all, it was Rossdale who earlier in the same week pressed for two rehearsals before the board of review on the Scheers' behalf; I believe Rossdale has now taken the further step of enlisting Senator Calder's assistance. Let's meet Calder.

William Calder. 1917. Library of Congress. Harris & Ewing Photograph

I give you William Musgrave Calder, Republican senator from New York, a Christian and an architect. As a young man, Calder took night classes at Cooper Union College and became a highly successful builder long before entering public office. It was Calder who developed the style of architecture known as "the two-family house" that dots the Brooklyn landscape to this day.

Calder is pro-immigrant. It is a political position that dovetails with his strong support of the building industry. Calder knows that immigrants comprise the backbone of the construction workforce. Before his election to the Senate in 1917, Calder served ten years in the US House of Representatives, during which time he consistently supported laws encouraging home ownership and opposing restrictions, like literacy test requirements, for the incoming Europeans who were likely to build those houses. That said, even Calder appears to have voted for the popular 1921 Emergency Quota Act.

When Senator Calder enters our narrative in October 1922, he is a first-term senator and, like Perlman and Rossdale, he is up for reelection on November 7. Here is the contemporary profile of Calder published by the *Woman Citizen:*

> William M. Calder (Republican), New York, is a master of the professional political manner. He practises [*sic*] the art of handshaking indefatigably. He is seldom seen without his coat-tails and his speeches are as sombre [*sic*] as his garb. On the floor, rather ineffectual. In his office, he meticulously attends to the work which tells the man back home that his Senator is continually at his service.

Well, on October 14, 1922, the Scheers become firsthand beneficiaries of Calder's "meticulous" service. What does Calder do after being called upon to help the Scheers? He immediately dispatches the Western Union telegram on the next page to Second Assistant Secretary Robe Carl White, asking if Meyer Scheer can be medically reexamined.

The request is denied. White telegrams Calder back two days later, on October 16, citing the absence of any evidence showing that Ellis Island doctors got it wrong:

> In absence [of] evidence showing incorrectness medical certificate Public Health Surgeons that Majer Scheer afflicted with valvular heart disease, Department does not feel justified in directing reexamination nor will any action be taken while habeas corpus proceedings pending.

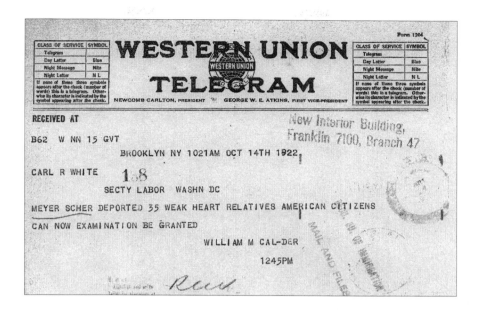

No new medical exam will occur. But there is a silver lining in White's telegram in that it at least confirms the Scheers will stay put at Ellis Island while legal proceedings remain pending in court.

October 16, 1922: Yet Another Political Gun Enters— This Time, Congressman Christopher D. Sullivan, a Democrat

Day 25 of Detention. On the same day that the request for medical reexamination is denied, something else happens: *bipartisanship.*

Up to this point, every elected politician who has helped the Scheers has been a Republican: Congressman Rossdale, Congressman Perlman, Senator Calder—all New York Republicans. But on October 16, a Democrat steps in, presumably at the beckoning of his Republican colleagues. And not just any Democrat, but Congressman

Christopher D. Sullivan, a Tammany Hall insider who used to chair the congressional committee in charge of the Department of Labor's budget. Let's meet him.

Christy Sullivan. 1905. Library of Congress. Harris & Ewing Photograph

This is Congressman Sullivan, known to friends and colleagues as Christy. Christy Sullivan is a New York City–born Irish American, Catholic school graduate who worked in real estate before joining Tammany Hall as a young man. Tammany Hall, in 1922, is still a mighty political machine controlling New York City Democratic Party politics and much of the city's affairs. By 1922, when he enters our story, Christy Sullivan has been in Congress for five years, and he has handily won reelection every two years with Tammany Hall backing. Back in 1917, when President Wilson was still in office, Christy Sullivan had chaired the congressional committee in charge of the Department of Labor's budget. (In 1922, Sullivan is in the minority party. Republicans control the presidency and both houses of Congress.) Sullivan too is up for reelection on November 7, 1922.

Although with Tammany Hall backing, Sullivan's reelection seems to be a certainty.

Here is what Congressman Sullivan does for the Scheers. On October 16, 1922, he writes to Commissioner-General of Immigration W. W. Husband, top officer of the US Bureau of Immigration (which sits within the Department of Labor and reports to Robe Carl White). Congressman Sullivan likely knows W. W. Husband personally. Here is an oddity: Sullivan sends his letter about the Scheers on the old stationery of the Sixty-Fifth Congress (1917–1919), which prominently (and outdatedly) identifies Sullivan as "Chairman" of the "House of Representatives Committee on Expenditures in the Department of Labor." Did he do this intentionally? By using this old letterhead, was Sullivan seeking to remind Husband of his past power over the Department of Labor's budget—power that could possibly be restored to Democrats in the next election, just a few weeks away? The letter crisply states:

My dear Mr. Husband:

With reference to the above case [of Meyer Scheer], I beg to state that the family of this man are willing to furnish bond in any amount in order that he may be permitted to enter this country and as I feel a personal interest in their welfare I am writing to ask that a reconsideration of the matter be had and it will be appreciated if you can issue an order permitting him to remain in this country.

Very truly yours,

C D Sullivan

Congressman Sullivan feels a *personal interest* in the welfare of Meyer Scheer's family? What explains this?

October 19, 1922: The Momentous Train Ride to Washington, DC

Day 28 of Detention. Three days after Congressman Sullivan has dispatched his letter, our band of politicians does one more thing—they arrange for a personal touch. They send an emissary to Washington: Walter Prendergast.

Walter Prendergast is a thirty-three-year-old Irish American Democrat from Brooklyn with Tammany Hall connections. Perhaps Congressman Sullivan (a Democrat) and Senator Calder (a Republican) met over a pub lunch in New York City to work out between them who best to dispatch for this assignment. The upshot is that they send Walter Prendergast (a Democrat) armed with a letter of introduction penned by Senator Calder (a Republican). Prendergast tucks Calder's letter of introduction into his coat pocket, boards the train at Grand Central Terminal, and heads to Washington for a one-on-one meeting with Department of Labor head Robe Carl White.

Remarkably, Senator Calder's letter of introduction survives in the Scheers' immigration file. Typed on Senate letterhead, it reads:

My dear Mr. White: This will introduce to you Mr. Walter Prendergast of Brooklyn, who is calling to see you concerning the immigration matter of Meyer Scheer, about which I wired you from New York a day or two ago. I am very deeply interested in this case, and am anxious that you should arrange for the alien's admission if it is at all possible. Mr. Prendergast will explain the details to you, and I appreciate any consideration you may extend the case.

Sincerely yours,
William M. Calder

Oh, how I long to know those "details"! Everything about this letter and Mr. Prendergast's trip is intriguing. Even just seeing Prendergast's name in the same sentence as Meyer Scheer's name—two total strangers to each other—is remarkable. And Senator Calder's words: "I am very deeply interested" in the case and "anxious" for Meyer Scheer's admission "if it is at all possible." Why?

The introduction letter is delivered and the meeting happens. There exists no record of what Prendergast and White discuss during their October 19, 1922 tête-à-tête. But whatever is said, whatever words Prendergast utters that day, they are words of salvation for my family. Because this in-person meeting is the clincher.

October 20, 1922: The Gates Open

Day 29 of Detention. One day after Prendergast's in-person meeting with White, the board of review convenes in Washington to reconsider the Scheers' appeal for a third time. This time, Congressman Rossdale is there *in person*. Attorney Gottlieb from HIAS is there too. Rossdale and Gottlieb both "are heard." Also put on the record: "Senator Calder, Congressmen Perlman and Sullivan, and Simon Wolf interested."

The hearing does not take long. Clearly, the board has received advanced instruction from Robe Carl White to approve the Scheers' admission. So the board merely summarizes the proceedings in the case and then dictates for the record:

> Subsequent to the foregoing Departmental orders [repeatedly affirming the Scheers' exclusion] representations have been made by Senator Calder and others which are of such character as may make it unlikely that these aliens, if admitted, will be become public charges.

Wherefore the Board of Review recommends that the foregoing Departmental orders affirming the excluding decision be rescinded; and that the appeals of the aliens be sustained, conditioned upon the filing of public charge bonds of $500 each for the husband and father, Majer Scheer; the wife and mother, Sura Blima; and the two children Rachel and Mirka, 9 and 13 respectively, with the usual school clause for Rachel and Mirka. The 17-year-old boy, Chaim, to be admitted outright.

Robe Carl White "so orders" the recommendation that same day. It is done. Ellis Island immigration authorities are notified. Louis Gottlieb gets word to HIAS's Ellis Island bureau. Subject to the bonds being signed, the Scheers will be admitted.

In pencil, someone handwrites at bottom of the order: "All interested parties notified. Write Sen. Calder 10/20/22."

October 24, 1922: "Duly Admitted" at Last

After thirty-three days in detention at Ellis Island, the Scheers' ordeal is over. On October 24, Uncle Jake comes to Ellis Island with two sureties who sign the Scheers' bonds. It is unclear why Uncle Jake himself did not or could not act as a surety, or what amount of debt the Greens took on to get these bonds signed by others. In any event, the sureties are Joseph Faden, a Bronx grocery business owner with reported net assets of $15,000, and David Flaxman, a Bronx furrier business owner with reported net assets of $35,000. Six bonds are signed in all, $500 each, totaling $3,000. Four are public charge bonds, for Meyer, Sura, Mirka, and Rachel. Titled "Bond That Alien Shall Not Become A Public Charge," they provide that should any of the four Scheers wind up on public welfare, the sureties will have to pay the guaranteed fine amount. The bonds further require the Scheers to report to immigration authorities every six months on their residence, occupation, and whether they have been inmates of any public institution. Hymie isn't subject to those requirements because he has been admitted outright. Additionally, two school bonds are signed for Mirka and Rachel, affirming that the girls will attend public school until they turn sixteen years of age.

Finally—after more than a month of detention at Ellis Island, and after the intervention of three congressmen, one senator, HIAS's chief lawyer, an elder Washington power broker, and a Mr. Walter Prendergast of Brooklyn—the Ellis Island clerk stamps their file "ADMITTED." The Scheers gather their luggage and leave Ellis Island with Uncle Jake. At last, they stand on the solid ground of the continental United States of America and begin their new lives.

October 25, 1922: Wrapping Up the Niceties

One day after the Scheers leave Ellis Island, Robe Carl White sends the letter on the following page to Senator Calder.

Tackling the *Why*

So that's what happened. It wasn't Aunt Annie on that train to DC; it was Walter Prendergast as emissary for New York politicians. It wasn't Calvin Coolidge who was persuaded to allow the Scheers in; it was Assistant Secretary of Labor Robe Carl White. Fascinating stuff. However, there is one gaping and obvious hole left in this historical narrative: the *why*. Why did the New York political community, at such high levels—Senator Calder, Congressmen Sullivan, Rossdale, and Perlman—rally behind the Scheers? I offer two theories for your consideration.

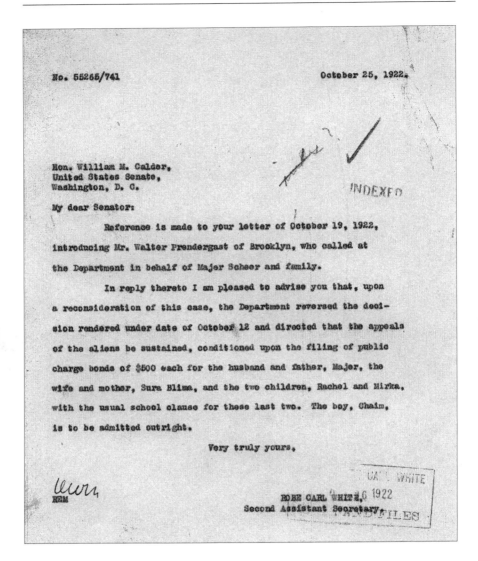

No. 55265/741   October 25, 1922.

Hon. William M. Calder,
United States Senate,
Washington, D. C.

My dear Senator:

Reference is made to your letter of October 19, 1922, introducing Mr. Walter Prendergast of Brooklyn, who called at the Department in behalf of Major Scheer and family.

In reply thereto I am pleased to advise you that, upon a reconsideration of this case, the Department reversed the decision rendered under date of October 12 and directed that the appeals of the aliens be sustained, conditioned upon the filing of public charge bonds of $500 each for the husband and father, Majer, the wife and mother, Sura Blima, and the two children, Rachel and Mirka, with the usual school clause for these last two. The boy, Chaim, is to be admitted outright.

Very truly yours,

ROBE CARL WHITE,
Second Assistant Secretary.

INDEXED

Theory One: It's a Horse, Not a Zebra

As my husband-the-doctor would tell you, medical students are trained to think of horses, not zebras, when they hear hoofbeats. In other words, don't go looking for an exotic diagnosis when a commonplace diagnosis fits and is far more likely to be true.

Applying this thinking, my first theory of the "why" is that New York politicians interceded to save the Scheers simply because this was good politics. *Business as usual, people; nothing special to see here.* After all, Congressman Rossdale was the Greens' local congressman and, in New York City in the 1920s, Republican and Democratic politicians alike courted popularity by serving the city's large immigrant population. Indeed, this kind of service was a key to Tammany Hall's power, as Congressman Christy Sullivan no doubt appreciated.

More than any other American city, New York City absorbed a massive number of immigrants during the Spigot Years. In 1900, New York City was the largest city in America *by a lot;* its population of 3.4 million was more than twice the population of America's next largest city, Chicago. By 1910, New York's population had swelled to approximately 4.8 million, a growth rate of 39 percent. Three-fourths of the city's population in 1910 were either immigrants or first-generation Americans. By 1920, the city's population had reached 5.6 million people, 36 percent of whom were foreign born.

Against this backdrop, providing excellent constituent service to the Greens—up-and-coming business owners who could vote and contribute to political campaigns—by helping the Greens' detained relatives was indeed good constituent politics. Add to that the pro-immigrant policies supported by many New York politicians, and Congressmen Rossdale and Perlman's further conviction to help Jews leave Europe, and it seems hardly surprising that New York politicians would step in to help the Greens and the Scheers.

Perhaps the best evidence of this "it-was-just-a-horse" theory comes from Secretary of Labor James Davis. On October 1, 1922, even as the Scheers sat in detention on Ellis Island, Secretary Davis sent his annual report to President Harding, in which he noted the annoying phenomenon of politicians interceding on behalf of detained immigrants. "Very frequently," Davis wrote the president, "Congressmen and Senators become interested on behalf of relatives of constituents, to the great embarrassment of enforcing officers as well as the Senators and Congressmen." Davis flagged the issue to buttress his department's proposal that immigration processing be shifted entirely away from domestic facilities like Ellis Island to the US consulates located abroad. As Davis advocated, not only would such an approach avoid the unfortunate circumstance of immigrants making the arduous transatlantic crossing only to be deemed ineligible once they arrived, but it would also eliminate the kerfuffle often raised by American citizens and local politicians following the detention of immigrant relatives already on US soil. (Eventually, Davis's proposal was followed by the US government, leading to Ellis Island's eventual closure in 1954.)

But just how frequently did politicians intercede on behalf of detained immigrants? It's hard to say, and there is no centralized system of records to tell us. Indeed, my understanding is that most immigration files from this era have either not survived or survived in skeletal fashion. Per my conversation with Ellis Island's head librarian, it's lucky and rare that the Scheers' immigration file survived complete with all those telegrams, letters, and hearing transcripts reflecting political intervention. Thus, even if someone were to go to the National Archives and undertake to review every still-existing immigration file of the early 1900s involving an appeal to the Department of Labor secretary's office, it might be impossible to gather accurate data about the frequency of political intervention. So we must take Secretary Davis at his word as relayed to President Harding, namely that by 1922 political intervention on behalf of detained immigrants occurred often enough to have become a real annoyance to his office.

It follows that New York politicians played an outsized role in annoying the Department of Labor. Think about it: Not only were the majority of detained immigrants physically held in New York City (at Ellis Island), but a great many of those had New York relatives sponsoring them. And with at least three quarters of their constituents composed of immigrants and first-generation Americans, New York politicians and their staffs must have been expert in immigration advocacy as a political necessity. Thus, when Secretary Davis vented in 1922 about the irksome lobbying of politicians on behalf of detained immigrants, more often than not, it would have been New Yorkers raising the ruckus.

So, maybe the story of how the Scheers managed to enter America is truly just a horse, not a zebra. To be sure, the Scheers' case was a tough one, due to Meyer's medical diagnosis. But in the end, it is likely that the story of the Scheers' entry into America is just a good example of how, in the early 1900s, New York's well-oiled political machine successfully leaned on the Department of Labor to admit immigrants whenever possible, in service of those politicians' constituents. If this "ordinary" explanation is the correct one, it is still extraordinary. The Scheers' case signifies that New York politicians of the era went to simply amazing lengths in the regular course of their duties to aid incoming immigrants. Furthermore, it shows that the fledgling department was responsive to such political outreach, however much annoyed by it, in exercising its discretion; and it exemplifies how different components of the US government pushed and pulled, and sometimes compromised, in enforcement of the nation's drastically changing immigration policy.

Theory Two: There's a Zebra Somewhere in This Barn

Perhaps I'm a bit dramatic, or maybe I just like zebras, because I am not fully convinced that good politics alone explains the "why" of the Scheers' story. Ellis Island sent thousands of people back to Europe every year, usually in excess of 5,000 per year. While that was a drop in the bucket compared to the hundreds of thousands of immigrants permitted to enter each year, it still meant that in any given year of this era—and particularly in 1922, following passage of the Emergency Quota Act—many thousands of immigrants were caught in Ellis Island's system of detentions and appeals, earning Ellis Island its nickname, the Isle of Tears. No matter how adept New York politicians may have been at helping their constituents' detained relatives, would they have gone as far as they did for the Scheers in every case? I am skeptical.

Saving the Scheers required more than a politician making a phone call to express "interest." It went beyond the sending of a telegram or just one letter. Multiple New York politicians engaged on the Scheers' behalf, in an escalating and sustained effort. A congressman's secretary was dispatched to advocate before the Department of Labor's Board of Review; a senator's emissary was sent to "explain the details" of the Scheers' case in person to the top labor official overseeing immigration. Republicans enlisted the help of a Democrat. Congressman Rossdale showed up *in person* to the Scheers' last appeals hearing. So while I could certainly be wrong, my gut tells me there was more to it, that someone had a special connection or a string to pull and pulled it on behalf of the Scheers.

Could Uncle Jake have had special influence with Congressman Rossdale? Sure, Jake Green was doing well with his garment business, but he didn't hold any political power or serious wealth. Jake didn't even gain his US citizenship until 1920, and he was a Bronx apartment renter who didn't even have a personal bank account. But perhaps Jake knew Congressman Rossdale personally. Who knows, maybe they attended the same synagogue, or Jake had made all of the congressman's suits. Or maybe this is where Aunt Annie came in as "the savior," which would support the legend Marion told. Maybe it was Annie, the only native New Yorker among the Greens, who had a personal connection to Congressmen Rossdale or Perlman. That still wouldn't explain why Senator Calder and Congressman Sullivan jumped in with urgency, to support the Scheers as they did, but it would be a start. Or could Joseph Scheer, Meyer's brother about whom we know practically nothing, have had a connection?

I've further wondered whether a payoff of some sort could have been involved. You never know. That said, there is nothing to indicate that the Greens had the means to pay a political bribe or that these politicians were on the take. If anything, the involvement of so many politicians in the Scheers' case makes that possibility less likely. Moreover, at the Department of Labor, the Scheers' immigration file is remarkable for its transparency. All of the outreach by the politicians to labor officials, all the letters and telegrams, even Walter Prendergast's visit to Robe Carl White, went through regular channels and was openly recorded and stamped for the Scheers' official immigration file.

At bottom, if there is a zebra lurking—to explain why multiple New York politicians intervened in the Scheers' case in the extraordinary way they did—it remains well camouflaged. An unsolved piece of the detective story. Purely for entertainment purposes, I end this chapter by offering two fictional movie plots to explain the "secret why," in Hollywood style that Marion would have loved. But first, let's stick to reality and see what became of the politicians who saved the Scheers by securing their future in America.

What Happened to the Politicians Who Saved the Scheers?

Congressman Albert Rossdale. I feel a special gratitude to Congressman Rossdale for never giving up on the Scheers' case. It was Rossdale who sent his secretary twice to Washington, DC, for the Scheers' appellate hearings. And when that wasn't enough, it was Rossdale whom I believe enlisted Senator Calder's help at the grimmest hour. And just a few weeks before election day, when his time should have been spent campaigning in the Bronx, it was Rossdale who personally attended the final board of review hearing in Washington on October 20, 1922, to ensure the Scheers' admission into the United States.

Congressman Rossdale lost his reelection bid on November 7, 1922. As a one-term congressman, helping the Scheers was one of his last acts of office. He tried running for office a few more times, unsuccessfully, and ultimately returned to the wholesale jewelry business and moved to Westchester. Albert Rossdale never married and had no children. He died in 1968 and is buried in Maimonides Cemetery, in Elmont, New York (about twenty minutes from my home).

I recently visited Albert Rossdale's grave, on a cold sunny day, to pay my respects. His grave seems a bit lonely, to be honest. Having no spouse or children, he was buried by a nephew, with a modest headstone that makes no mention of his time in Congress. It simply notes that he died at the age of eighty-nine and was a beloved uncle. By my family, he shall be remembered.

Congressman Nathan David Perlman. Congressman Perlman, who early on expressed "interest" in the Scheers' case, went on to win his reelection bid in November 1922. Perlman served in Congress until 1927, for a total of four terms.

After leaving Congress, Perlman returned to the practice of law and remained civically engaged. He served as vice president of Beth Israel Hospital and as a New York City magistrate, running unsuccessfully for New York State attorney general in 1936. Perlman also played a pivotal role in speaking out against anti-Semitism in America. In 1927, as vice president of the American Jewish Congress, Perlman helped lead a public response to the virulent anti-Semitic diatribes of automobile magnate Henry Ford. Later, in the late 1930s, Perlman worked to disrupt anti-Semitic rallies organized in New York City by the German American Bund, a pro-Nazi organization.

Perlman died in 1952 at the age of sixty-two. He is buried at Mount Hebron Cemetery in Queens, where his understated yet compelling gravestone reads, "Jurist. Legislator. Humanitarian. . . . His life was full of kind words and gentle deeds." A Manhattan street abutting Beth Israel Hospital—Nathan Perlman Place—is named in his honor.

Senator William Musgrave Calder. Oh, how Senator Calder's words intrigue me—"I am very deeply interested in this case, and am anxious that you should arrange for the alien's admission if it is at all possible. Mr. Prendergast will explain the details to you."

Two weeks after the Scheers were admitted into the United States, Senator Calder lost his reelection bid. Helping the Scheers was one of his last acts of office, as it was for Congressman Rossdale.

After leaving the Senate, Calder returned to his construction business and remained active in Republican political circles, becoming president of the National Republican Club. He died in Brooklyn on his seventy-sixth birthday on March 3, 1945. His funeral was attended by hundreds of dignitaries and constituents. His obituary in the *New York Times* reads:

Though best known for his activities in Republican politics and his public service, Mr. Calder was credited with having done more during the last thirty years for the growth of his home borough than anyone else. He built at least 3,500 homes and took the lead in the real estate development of the Park Slope, Windsor Terrace, Flatbush, and Sheepshead Bay sections of Brooklyn.

Calder's two-family houses dot the Brooklyn landscape to this day, and a street in Park Slope—Calder Place—bears his name. Calder is buried in Green-Wood Cemetery in Brooklyn, next to his wife.

Congressman Christopher Sullivan. Congressman Sullivan, who leveraged his influence to help the Scheers and, I believe, tapped Walter Prendergast to go to Washington, DC, handily won reelection on the Democratic ticket and went on to serve nineteen more years in Congress. Reportedly, in his more than two decades in Congress, Sullivan never made a single speech on the House floor. This was a man who understood the value of getting things done out of public view, not in front of a crowd.

Ultimately, near the end of his life, Sullivan was named "boss" of Tammany Hall in 1937, though by this time Tammany Hall's power had been substantially weakened by scandal and a changing political landscape led by New York City's "reform" mayor, Fiorello La Guardia. Sullivan passed away in 1942 and is buried in Calvary Cemetery in Woodside, Queens, his name added last to a family tombstone.

Walter Prendergast. I doubt any of the Scheers ever heard of Walter Prendergast's name or knew the pivotal role he played in their salvation, by taking that train ride in October 1922 to meet with Robe Carl White. A couple of years later, in 1924, Walter Prendergast was named a deputy sheriff for the Brooklyn District Attorney's Office. He served in that office for forty years, rising to chief investigator, before retiring in 1964 at the age of seventy-seven. The *New York Times* article marking his retirement described Prendergast as "a chunky bulldog of a man, with steely blue eyes," further reporting that Prendergast had served eight sheriffs and five district attorneys since 1924. Prendergast died in 1979 and is buried in Holy Cross Cemetery in Brooklyn. Here is a photo of Prendergast with his grandson, circa 1947, courtesy of the Prendergast family.

Walter Prendergast and grandson. Circa 1947.
Courtesy Prendergast family

Simon Wolf. One of the most influential Jewish American advocates of his era, Simon Wolf also lent his name to the Scheers' case, a gesture of his lifelong commitment to help Jews thrive in America. In June 1923, eight months after the Scheers finally gained admittance to the United States, Wolf died at the age of eighty-six. He is buried in the Washington Hebrew Congregation Cemetery in Washington, DC.

Robe Carl White. Lastly, I pay tribute to Robe Carl White, the second assistant secretary of labor whose ultimate decision it was to authorize the Scheers' admission into the United States. This is White.

Robe Carl White. 1925. Library of Congress.
National Photo Company Collection

I regard White as an honest actor doing his best at a sensitive time in our nation's immigration history. White and his colleagues had to guide a young federal agency, founded only one decade earlier, through two of the most tumultuous issues of the day: the rising labor movement and changing immigration policy. While strictly enforcing the 1921 immigration quotas, the Department of Labor at this time also worked to improve conditions at Ellis Island, to prevent shipping companies from preying on vulnerable immigrants, and to ensure due process for those ordered excluded.

In the Scheers' case, while I am hardly unbiased, Robe Carl White made the right call. To be sure, absent high-level and repeated intervention by New York politicians, White would have stood by Ellis Island's field decision and the Scheers would have been sent back to Europe. But with the strong support of established American relatives and the vouching of numerous elected officials, the Scheers were, indeed, a good bet for America. Meyer Scheer had a trade and had never missed a day of work on account of his recently detected heart murmur; his son, Hymie, likewise was skilled and ready to work. All the Scheers were literate, and they were highly motivated to become US citizens. Whatever Walter Prendergast said to White during their tête-à-tête (and, oh, how I wish we knew), at the end of the day, any risk posed by admitting the Scheers was low, and White ultimately exercised his broad discretion accordingly.

White appears to have remained at the Department of Labor until 1933, at which time the Democratic administration of Franklin D. Roosevelt took over the executive branch. I have been unable to locate information about how White spent the rest of his life or where he is buried.

Foray into Fiction: Two Proposed Hollywood Movie Plots about the Secret *Why*

Now, let's have some fun. With the historical narrative faithfully laid out, it is time for imaginative filling in the blanks. I give you two proposed movie plots: a love story and an organized crime story.

Movie Plot One: The Love Story

Congressman Albert Rossdale's first love—the unrequited love of his life and, as it turned out, the only love of his life—was Annie. Years before she became "Anna Green," the wife of Louis Green, or anyone's Aunt Annie, she was Albert's Annie. She and Albert had grown up together in New York, neighbors on the same block. He'd loved her since the second grade. Annie was not going to win any beauty pageant, but she was slender and pretty and direct, and she spoke beautifully. She was more comfortable in her own skin than any girl he knew.

He courted her in their late teens, after graduating from high school, when he had the boosted confidence of a paying job. At age nineteen, Albert was lucky enough to have procured a coveted, full-time clerk position at the post office, and he had the pocket money to show for it. He would take Annie out for an ice cream every Thursday. Sometimes they would sit in the park on Sunday.

Albert never fully recovered from the day Annie came to see him at the post office loading dock to tell him that she was soon to be married to Louis Green, a young garment industry worker. Louis was an immigrant from Galicia and she had fallen in love with him, she told Albert modestly and matter-of-factly, in her way. Oh, sure, Albert knew that it was common for eligible girls to be courted by a number of men at the same time. But how had he lost Annie to a greenhorn? His Annie? Albert was too well-mannered and dumbfounded to protest. He kissed her hand goodbye, wished her well, and hoped she wouldn't notice his eyes welling up behind his spectacles.

Albert never married. He never had children. He left the post office several years later to make money in his family's jewelry business and then made a run at politics. The all-consuming work of politics was a salve for his loneliness.

The next time Albert saw Annie after that morning at the loading dock was in late September 1922. *Congressman,* his staffer told him, *there is a lady here to see you. She doesn't have an appointment but says her name is Annie and that it's urgent. . . .*

The sight of Annie after all those years; oh, how his eyes took it in hungrily. She had the meatier frame now of a mother, and her hair was pinned back. She looked, well, lovely. She needed his help, she said, coming right to the point, as always. *It's for my husband's sister, Albert. She is stuck in detention at Ellis Island, about to be sent back to*

Europe on account of some heart murmur they found in her husband that no one even knew about until now. Three young, beautiful children, Albert. I've seen them myself. The family is desperate, she explained, and the petition to the Board of Special Inquiry already denied. *Oh, Albert, is there anything you can do?* The unspoken subtext: "Oh, Albert, I know how deeply I wounded you all those years ago, choosing Louis over you. But look at what an important man you've become since. A congressman! I do hope that makes you feel better about things. Albert, please, could you find it in yourself to set aside the old hurt and help us?"

Annie needed him. He would spare no effort.

Movie Plot Two: The Organized Crime Story

Back in the old country, Joseph Scheer was always a violent boy and a strong one. Of her five sons, this was the son over whom Joseph's mother prayed the most. Joseph (or Yossel, as he was called in Europe) carried around too much anger, which he relieved by pummeling other boys in Kopyczynce over slights both real and imagined. There was no chance of Joseph going to work in a butcher shop, day in and day out, like his father or brothers.

Still, Joseph never intended to kill the tailor's son. They were just tussling. Joseph shoved the boy hard and the boy fell backward, accidentally hitting his head on a jagged stone. The skull opened like a gourd. Joseph watched, stunned. He was fifteen. He ran.

Only one person saw Joseph before he disappeared from Kopyczynce forever. His older brother, Meyer. Somehow, Meyer found Joseph that night, even when the police could not, hiding out in the brush. Meyer confirmed that news of the death was everywhere and that police were at their parents' house waiting for Joseph's return. In Galicia, Jews did not regard police officers as people who were there to help; a police officer was someone who could cut your head off. *Cross the Zbruch river,* Meyer urged Joseph in a quiet voice. *Go over to the Russian side before the sun rises. You are strong. You can find a way.* Even Meyer, his gentle brother, saw no point in trying to persuade Joseph to stay. *Here, take this.* From his coat pockets, Meyer produced two rolls, a raw potato, three apples, and a handful of kronen. The two brothers embraced for the last time.

Joseph never forgot Meyer's kindness. Not when Joseph snuck onto a Russian cargo ship and then onto the English cargo ship that brought him to New York in 1907 as a stowaway; not when Joseph scrounged for food on the Lower East Side like an alley cat and started to steal what he needed; and not as Joseph rose through the ranks of New York City's Jewish underworld and became the trusted associate of Arnold "the Brain" Rothstein, a mob kingpin.

Pretextually, Joseph worked in the garment industry, like practically everyone else did. But bootlegging, loansharking, bookmaking, and violence—those were Joseph's real trades. Joseph spoke English fluently, but in public he spoke in Yiddish, pretending to speak only a broken English. It was yet another layer of protective armor. Yes, Joseph was in good with Rothstein, with the Prohibition gangs, with the up-and-coming Meyer Lansky and Lucky Luciano. Hell, Joseph had even been in good with Harry "Gyp the Blood" Horowitz, that is, until Harry was sent to the electric chair in 1914 for murder of a government witness. Joseph's discretion (he was never flashy) matched his talents. While the Jewish and Italian underworld didn't completely run New York City, whatever the mob didn't run, Tammany Hall did. Yes, the mob and Tammany Hall got along just fine. The way Joseph saw it, the things that needed to get done got done and everyone was better off for it.

In September 1922, one of Joseph's assignments by day was to review the daily ship manifests for the incoming passengers arriving in New York Harbor. Luciano had asked him to keep watch for the arrival of certain rivals from Italy. Immigration inspectors were paid off, naturally, for such access. And that's when Joseph saw it . . . the entry in the SS *Berengaria* manifest for a "Majer Scheer" from Kopyczynce, arriving with a wife and three children. Meyer!

Their reunion occurred on September 26, when Joseph showed up at Ellis Island, completely unexpected, to testify at Meyer's special inquiry hearing. Meyer's shock was surpassed only by his joy. But there was no time then to catch up, they were being ushered into the hearing room already. . . .

Fast-forward to Joseph sitting in the office of Arnold Rothstein on October 13, 1922. Rothstein, behind an enormous mahogany desk, wearing a three-piece suit and chewing on a cigar. That was Arnold Rothstein, civilized, a genius who ran organized crime like a corporation. *Arnold, I need a favor. My older brother is stuck at Ellis Island. I just found out. They've ordered him sent back to Europe. I need to find a way to get the decision reversed.* Rothstein locked eyes with Joseph for a moment and then nodded. Rothstein called out to his secretary, *Rose, get me Tammany Hall on the line.*

☎

A Telephone Call: January 1993

Lisa: Grandma, I'm calling to thank you again for making me those *kichelah*. I took them back to school with me. They are so delicious.

Marion: Oh, they tasted good? Good. I couldn't taste them because my teeth don't work. But what is the sense complaining? When women used to go into my brother's butcher store and complain that the chicken smelled, Hymie would say, "Lady, if I turn you over and put you on the table, you think you'd smell any better?"

CHAPTER FOUR

Coming of Age in America

The Cat's Pajamas

I N BROOKLYN, I BECAME A DIFFERENT person entirely. Everyone called me Marion, like Marion Davies, the 1920s movie star. I learned to dress and pose for the camera and bat my eyes by copying the glamorous actresses of Hollywood. I wore my hair in a mannish bob, and I wore shorts to show off my legs, and red lipstick. I became an expert on the latest styles. Even my name was glamorous: Marion Scher, like an actress. Oh, how I loved those days! Being young in New York City in the 1920s. Here, let me show you some pictures of myself.

Oh, I had loads of girlfriends, and all the boys chased me—what wasn't there to love? It was a time of excitement. But, ah, I am getting ahead of myself again. Let me tell you how we came to live in Brooklyn.

The Gifts of a Plucked Chicken

So after all the commotion at Ellis Island, my father's heart murmur never gave him any trouble. When we left Ellis Island, first we went home with Uncle Jake to the Bronx. After a few weeks, my father found work as a delivery boy for another butcher and Hymie took a job in a slaughterhouse. Uncle Jake helped us to rent a few rooms on the Lower East Side. That's where we started out, living on the Lower East Side

138

in a tenement on East Houston and Norfolk Streets. Later we rented a small apartment on Grand Street, near Ratner's restaurant.

Within a year's time, Uncle Jake gave my father the money to open his own butcher shop on the Lower East Side. My mother worked in the store too, plucking feathers from the chickens. It made her asthma worse, but what could she do? My parents needed to work. Those plucked chickens put food on our table.

Ruthie and I went to public school on the Lower East Side. Ruthie took to it right away. She learned to speak English with a beautiful diction, and the teachers pushed her ahead in classes very fast. "Rapid advance," they called it. Also, Aunt Annie took Ruthie under her wing—I think my aunt wanted to adopt Ruthie for her own daughter. All the school vacations, Ruthie went to live with Aunt Annie. Soon, Ruthie sounded and acted American born, very refined. She was quiet and lovely, my sister, with skin like snow.

Of course I learned English too and arithmetic and writing in school, but I didn't take to it like Ruthie. Every day, I used to leave class and go to the teacher's lounge and make coffee for all the teachers with extra cream and sugar and take it to them. Oh, how they loved my coffee. "Marion," they would say, "nobody makes a coffee like you." What I really wanted was to work, like Hymie. And so I left school after the sixth grade. But even after that, I went every Tuesday afternoon to "continuation school" for a few more years.

Brooklyn Bound

My father's first butcher shop failed because there was too much competition on the Lower East Side. But Uncle Jake, our angel, helped out my father one more time—to open a second store, this time in Brooklyn, on Osborne Street. Thank God, the second store was a success.

Hymie and Mama worked in the store too, and we all moved to Brooklyn, to the Brownsville section. So many Jewish people were moving from Manhattan to Brownsville in those days that it was practically as crowded as the Lower East Side, buzzing all the time. We lived at 40 Watkins Street, near Pitkin Avenue. At least now we had our own toilet in the apartment. That's when we took in Mitzi, a stray cat. Mitzi was so smart she did her business on the toilet like a human, honest to God.

Blossoming

I didn't get my period until age sixteen. My mama took me around to all the big doctors to find out what was wrong with me, and they couldn't find a thing. Finally it came, and then I developed the biggest bosom. And I had small pearly white teeth and two adorable dimples. I was the cutest thing, if I have to say so myself.

I went to work in a chemical company as a saleslady. That was my first job. There we sold all kinds of chemicals, and downstairs, hidden in the basement, the bosses were mixing whiskey to sell on the black market. It was Prohibition and you couldn't sell or buy liquor out in the open. The bosses told me if a policeman came by the store, I should just smile and act normal. They kept a Great Dane named Kiwa guarding the shop. That dog was so big, it could take your head off with one bite. But I became friends with Kiwa and soon Kiwa wanted only me to feed him. When the business was closed on Sunday, I still went to the store to feed the dog.

One summer, my father took us to the Catskills for a few weeks to see if it would help Mama's asthma to be out of the city in the fresh air. Brooklyn was like an oven in the summer. You could fry an egg on the cement. Up in the Catskill Mountains there were farms and lakes. That's where Jewish people would go in the summer to escape the heat.

Such memories I have of that Catskills trip! I sang and danced and did all the girls' makeup. No one could draw an eyebrow with a pencil like me. I told jokes about Mae West that had them laughing on the floor. And I won the Charleston competition. "C'mon, Marion, give us a smile! Let's see those dimples," the boys used to tease me. Ah, to be young and alive is the best thing.

Back home, the boys lined up to take me out. I was a very good girl and the boys always came to the house first to meet my parents. One boy, Irving, brought Mama an expensive tablecloth. Mama liked that. Another boy, Willy, a friend of Hymie's, had such bad hair, sticking straight up, that one time when he came to take me out, I pretended to be sick and I hid under the blankets. Once, a man proposed marriage to me on a train ride to Saratoga after talking to me for only an hour. I felt like the cat's pajamas.

Meeting Emanuel

I won't keep you, you've heard enough of my stories already. But before you go, let me tell you how I came meet my husband, Emanuel Zornberg.

For years, I was single and enjoying myself. I lived with my parents in the apartment on Watkins Street. I did most of the cooking and cleaning, since Mama was sick much of the time. I didn't mind. To be busy is the best thing. Four-thirty every morning, I woke up to cook breakfast for my father and Hymie before they left for the butcher store. I made their lunches too. And I would take my parents around town, to doctors and wherever they needed to go, to help interpret, since their English was not too good.

Life was wonderful in New York. About five or six years after we came to America, Hymie got married to my good friend, Helen. Ruthie graduated from high school and went to work for the East New York Savings Bank, keeping the books. She had a good kup [head] on her. And when I wasn't working, I went to see all the talking pictures with my friends, so we could examine the Hollywood stars and learn the latest styles.

Believe me, I could have married very young if I wanted, and I could have married a rich man. I had lots of chances. But I married a smart man instead. Can you believe it?—My Manny (which is how I called Emanuel) came from Husiatyn, the same town as us in the old country. Actually, our fathers were both butchers in Husiatyn. His parents knew my parents before the First World War.

I met Manny at a *lantzman* ball in 1931, during the Depression. Back in those days, Jews in America who came from the same towns of Europe called each other lantzmen. The lantzmen would form societies to help one another. Many things those societies did for their people in America, and they held dances and parties, in a synagogue or a dance

hall, to get everyone together. It was at such a ball that Manny asked me to dance. He claimed he remembered me from when I was a little girl in Husiatyn. He was dressed very smart in his suit. And I liked the way he held me on the dance floor, confident.

A beautiful Yiddish he spoke and a beautiful English too. So smart Manny was and handsome with broad shoulders. Back in

Europe as a boy, Manny worked in a mill, lifting heavy sacks of flour. That's how come he got those broad shoulders. Here, look at this photo of Manny as a young man still in Europe, from the early 1920s.

You can tell just from his eyes that he is very intelligent. Manny spoke ten languages that he taught himself. When he was a teenager, all the townspeople in Europe had him write their letters in English to America.

Manny came to America later than I did, in 1927, alone, without his parents or brother or sisters, when he was twenty-six years of age. He got very lucky. I think he must have impressed the officers at the US consulate, because America was taking almost no one from Poland in those days. But they let him have a visa. Manny's Uncle Eli in New York then took him into business to learn the furrier trade. Emanuel started out skinning skunks in a factory in Manhattan. From there, he learned to sew and cut garments and to make beautiful coats from mink and beaver and Persian lamb. Whatever money he made, Manny sent back to Europe to help his family, and to help his sisters and brother buy passage to go to Canada, which still had some loopholes to let in people from Europe.

As soon as Manny came to America—this is before I met him—he took night classes and they gave him his high school diploma in one year. He had the head of a philosopher. He knew more than the teachers, actually. Later, when Manny was courting me, I would stand over his shoulder and admire his writing. And he would look up at me and say, "Mirinyu, God sent you to me."

We were married on June 12, 1932, right in the middle of the Depression. I'll show you our wedding picture:

Manny had another uncle in New York who was a rabbi, Feter Nuchem Wexler [*feter* means uncle in Yiddish], and he married us in a small ceremony. It was a terrible time of people being out of work, and the worst time to be a furrier—who had money to buy fur coats? We had hardly anything to live on, so Manny and I lived with my parents and Ruthie, all squeezed into that small apartment on Watkins Street. I like to say that we lived on love in those years. We did. We lived on love.

So Now You Know

To my great-grandchildren, and my great-great nieces and nephews, now you know how you came to be in America. I've told you how Uncle Jake sent us the tickets to come over when I was a little girl, and how the doctor discovered my father's heart murmur at Ellis Island, and how Aunt Annie saved the family by convincing President Coolidge to let us in. There is nothing else to tell.

But I do want to give you a few pieces of advice for going out on dates. For the boys, listen to me, it doesn't matter if you have the face of a Clark Gable. But it's very important for a man to be clean looking and to dress nicely. So before you go out, make sure to comb your hair and put on a nice shirt and coat. Trust me, this will make a difference. And for the girls, forget this nonsense of wanting to diet, diet, diet all the time. Take it from me, the worst thing is to be homely looking, like a plucked chicken. Darling, the best thing is to be pleasingly plump. Never was I so fat and beautiful as when I finally had my son, Ira—my face simply beamed. Listen to me, if you gain a few pounds, it means you're happy, that's all. And if you get too fat, then just eat less sweets and stay away from the rye bread and butter.

ENTER: THE HISTORY DETECTIVE (FOR THE LAST TIME)

Return to Ellis Island

Marion and her family—now the Scher family—returned to Ellis Island once after being admitted to the United States in October 1922. Marion never breathed a word of it, but the records unearthed at the National Archives bear witness to the visit. It occurred on June 24, 1924, nineteen months following their admission. Aunt Annie accompanied them on the ferry. Going back to Ellis Island must have given them the heebie-jeebies, except that it was their own request that triggered the visit: They wanted to prove that Marion was *older* than her immigration records reflected—already past sixteen years of age—and thus old enough to be released from her school bond. Marion wanted to work. And she needed the US authorities' official permission before leaving school. No wonder Marion never mentioned this trip—it had to do with her age.

Things went well for the family this time at Ellis Island. The assistant commissioner sent this report to immigration headquarters the following day:

> This family who arrived here September 1922, were admitted under public charge bonds with school clauses for the children, the seventeen year old son Chaim being admitted outright.
>
> Recently there has been submitted through the Bureau of Attendance, New York City, an abstract from the records of births, showing that Mirka Scheer, who it was stated was thirteen years of age in 1922, was in fact born July 15th, 1907. Waiver of the school clause in this bond was requested but in order that proper consideration may be given to the case, the family were directed to appear here, which they did yesterday. The husband and father who was certified to be afflicted with valvular disease of the heart has been able to support his family since their arrival here. Up to six months ago he was employed in a butcher shop but at that time purchased his own business, which he now conducts and which he claims is worth $1,000.
>
> The son Hyman earns from $20 to $30 weekly and the father averages from $50 to $70 per week from his business. The family make a good appearance and there is no doubt in my mind that the child Mirka is at least seventeen years of age. The younger child, Ruchel, is probably nearer thirteen than eleven, although no certificate in her case has been presented.

The aunt who accompanied the aliens stated that there is no intention of sending Mirka to work, but she may do so if she so desires and continue her studies at evening school.

Ha!—"There is no doubt in my mind that the child Mirka is at least seventeen years of age"—Marion must have batted her eyes at the poor man. According to the birth record presented, Marion had been born in 1907, which would have made her fifteen years old when she first arrived at Ellis Island in 1922. Her school bond was promptly canceled.

Becoming Americans

What happened thereafter is a story that has repeated itself millions of times over in America. The Schers, like so many immigrants before them and since, assimilated into American life. The children picked up English and American culture in what seemed like the blink of an eye (although Hymie and Marion never fully lost their accents the way Ruthie did), and the parents worked hard to make a living, sticking close to their immigrant community and struggling to learn enough English to get by. The Schers remained kosher and observant of Jewish holidays (Sarah even continued to go to the mikvah), but within a matter of months, Marion was swept up in the excitement and fashion of the Roaring Twenties, of life in New York City, wearing cosmetics and shorts, and going to the movies. Even if Meyer and Sarah had tried to stop her, they never stood a chance.

Their former small-town life in Galicia became a distant memory as the Schers plugged themselves into the urban New York City economy—Hymie becoming a butcher shop owner, like his father; Marion a saleslady; Ruthie a bookkeeper. Marion eventually left the chemical company and went to work at Mayrock's, the high-end home furnishing store in Brownsville where the brides and well-to-do ladies came to pick out their china patterns. Marion was Mayrock's top saleslady for years.

In 1933 and 1934, all of the Schers became naturalized United States citizens.

The Deepening of Roots amid Tumultuous Times

In Brooklyn, the Schers struggled through the Great Depression like everyone else, and got by. Hymie and his wife, Helen, had two children, Ronald (Ronnie) and Rosalind (Rozzie). Marion and Emanuel, cramped in that Watkins Street apartment with Marion's parents, could not conceive a child for the first seven years of marriage. Then, in 1939, Marion and Emanuel finally moved into their own apartment and, voilà, within two weeks Marion became pregnant. On December 31, 1939, shortly before midnight, Marion and Emanuel welcomed into the world their first and only child, my father, Ira. He weighed more than ten pounds at birth and was delivered by emergency cesarean section. "Take him home in a high chair!" the nurses exclaimed, as Marion retold it. Ira's birth was a great joy during a tumultuous time. Four months earlier, Adolph Hitler had invaded Poland.

And so it was that, just twenty years after Marion and her family had been refugees of the First World War, another world war now gripped the earth. Sixteen million Americans went off to fight the Axis powers, including 550,000 Americans of the Jewish faith. More than 60 percent of all Jewish American doctors served in the war. Defeating the Nazis was a moral imperative for the United States. What's more, most Jewish Americans still had relatives in

Eastern Europe, now trapped in Nazi-controlled territory. Emanuel's beloved older sister, Raisa, was in Poland with her husband and three children, in the town of Chorostkov, near Husiatyn. Elka Scheer and her eight children (many of whom had spouses and children of their own by this time), the cousins who had sheltered Marion's family during the First World War, were still in Kopyczynce. What would become of them?

Like everyone else, the Schers celebrated D-Day and the eventual German surrender. And they awoke to the incomprehensible news that followed the liberation of the concentration and labor camps in Nazi-occupied territories. Emanuel learned that his sister had been murdered by the Nazis, along with her husband and children. They learned that the Scheers of Kopyczynce, their dear cousins, had all perished in the camps—save Kayla and Etka, the two youngest of Abraham and Elka Scheer's children. That any relative had survived was a drop of grace in an ocean of despair. What dark days those were, even amid the Allied victory, of trying to make sense of humanity and God, and trying to locate and reconnect with survivors. Mass murder on a scale so colossal, how could one make sense of it? One million Jewish children marched into gas chambers. Three million Jews murdered in Poland alone.

Gradually, the individual stories of death and survival emerged. A Jewish survivor from the town of Chorostkov—where Emanuel's sister, Raisa, had lived—found Emanuel in Brooklyn after the war. He relayed how, first, the Jewish residents of the town had been confined to a ghetto and then how, on erev Rosh Hashanah in 1943, the Nazis came to the ghetto with a roving gas van. The Nazis had considered this vehicle, equipped with a mobile gas chamber, to be a great technological innovation—because now, instead of lining

Jewish people up and shooting them in the street, they could neatly load fifty or a hundred people at a time into the van and drive them to a burial pit where the cargo would be dead upon arrival of carbon monoxide poisoning. This man described how he had hidden in an attic to escape the gas van that day, but how Raisa and her family were sadly among those loaded onto it. Emanuel never came to terms with his sister's murder. It was a fresh pain his whole life. And I was named in her memory—Raisa is my middle name.

Kayla and Etka, the only two surviving Scheer cousins, eventually came to America after the war from a displaced persons camp in Europe. They described how in Kopyczynce, even before the Nazi invasion, Jews had been so economically ostracized that it was nearly impossible to earn a living. Along with their mother and brothers, they had operated the only kosher butcher shop that was allowed to stay open in the town. On Fridays, they would roast chickens and bake challahs and deliver them to the town's poorest, starving Jewish families for Shabbos dinner. But when the Nazis descended upon Kopyczynce in the 1940s, Jewish residents were killed on contact or sent to labor camps. Kayla and Etka had been rounded up for deportation to a camp when a Ukrainian officer, who knew Kayla from town, spotted her in the line with her younger sister. "I'm going to turn my back," he told Kayla, "run and don't look back." Kayla and Etka ran. That act of kindness spared their lives. The two sisters survived the Second World War by hiding under haystacks in the barns of righteous Christian families and in the stable of a church.

In 1945, the Scher family also buried Meyer. Meyer's heart had always remained strong, but he died from cancer at the age of sixty-nine. Marion had nursed her father in his final months. After he passed away, his widow, Sarah, moved in with Marion, Emanuel, and Ira. Sarah lived ten more years.

But, oh, there were blessings too; so many blessings for the Schers. Life went on as it must, and postwar America was booming. Marion's sister, Ruthie, who had married George Levine during the war, named their first daughter—Myra—after Meyer. A second daughter, Joan (Joanie), followed. Sarah lived long enough to ensure that her grandson, Ira, with whom she lived, spoke a fluent Yiddish. They lived to see Israel become a state in 1948. And whenever Marion and her brother Hymie were together in a room, a spark of life and humor and music ran through it. There was singing and dancing and piano playing. Hymie's son, Ronnie, and Ira had both inherited the Scher musical gene. Ronnie became a professional bandleader. Ira entertained more than 200 guests on the accordion at his bar mitzvah (and years later, again, at my wedding).

Emanuel, Marion's husband, remained in the furrier trade. Each morning, he would travel to work at the factory in a shirt and tie, remove them during the long and sweaty workday of cutting skins and nailing coats, and return home in his shirt and tie. With months of seasonal unemployment in the fur line, Marion worked a series of jobs throughout her life to help make ends meet. That was just fine with her. Marion always liked to work and took pride in the compliments she received in every job she held. In the off-season, Emanuel opened a business in one room of their apartment, making custom-designed ladies' fur coats, which Marion modeled to attract customers, naturally. Emanuel's late nights were reserved for reading history and philosophy.

Ira, my dad, became the first of the family to graduate from college. He became a high school social studies teacher and assistant principal, proudly serving for forty-eight years in the New York City school system. He and my mother, Judith (a fellow Brooklyn College student and also a teacher), married and stayed in Brooklyn. They had five children and bought a house in Sea Gate, a housing community at the tip of Coney Island. The roots deepened.

Harvard Bound

In 1988, sixty-six years after my grandmother, Marion, stepped off the SS *Berengaria,* I arrived in Cambridge, Massachusetts, as a Harvard College freshman and moved into Pennypacker Hall. My roommate also had ancestors who had come to America by ship . . . the *Mayflower.* We became fast friends and were the odd and wonderful pair: she, a six-foot-one rower from Wisconsin who became cocaptain of the winning Harvard women's crew team, and I, a five-foot-one Brooklynite with a rambunctious sense of humor who enjoyed doing historical research.

Within my first month at Harvard, I had an experience that has always stayed with me, an example of what makes this country great. The instructor of our expository writing seminar assigned each of us to write a five-page narrative about ourselves. My fellow classmates in that seminar included a Kennedy and a Weld (of the Boston Brahmin Weld family and a close relative of then-Governor Weld of Massachusetts). I handed in a humor-inflected essay about the years I'd worked weekends and summers in high school as a meat wrapper at Glick's Kosher Meats in Brooklyn. (Hey, the apple doesn't fall far . . .). The essay earned top marks and, to my surprise, the instructor called on me to read it aloud in class. How exhilarated I felt, reading aloud my butcher shop escapades, at Harvard, entertaining all present, Kennedys and Welds included.

For all of its complexities, I ask you, where else but in America?

Jake Green, with his eldest daughter, Mona. Location unknown, circa 1940s.

Marion always called her Uncle Jake "their angel." He sponsored the Scheers' admission into the United States, sent them money for passage, and helped Marion's father, Meyer, open a successful butcher shop in Brooklyn.

A young Marion, about nineteen years old, posing in a sailor hat. Location unknown, circa 1925.

Judging by the greenery, this might have been taken during the Catskills trip when Marion did all the girls' makeup and won the Charleston dance competition.

154

Marion and Emanuel, young marrieds and gorgeous. Circa mid-1930s.

Taken in a professional studio, this photograph captures a charm our society has since lost—people posing for formal photos in their coats!

Marion, jubilant, with her infant son, Ira. Brooklyn, 1940.

My father's birth name was Isadore, and everyone called him Izzy. Years later, when he was about nine years old, Marion and Emanuel officially changed their son's name to Ira, to sound more American. In this photo, Marion sits outside a music store. Notice the guitar in the window priced at $4.95.

Sarah with her grandson, Ira. The Catskills, circa 1951.

Every morning of that summer trip, Ira escorted Sarah on a walk. By being close to her, Ira learned to speak a fluent Yiddish.

Sarah Scher (center) with Hymie and Ruthie (top row, right) and Helen (Hymie's wife) and Marion (bottom right). Marion and Emanuel's apartment in the Brownsville neighborhood of Brooklyn, circa mid-1950s.

Marion loved to host and whenever she and Hymie were together, there was laughter and singing.

Ruthie's daughters, Myra (age seventeen) and Joanie (age fifteen). Elmont, Long Island, 1962.

Their mother Ruthie, the youngest of the Scheers who arrived in America in 1922, had quickly picked up English and become Americanized. Myra and Joanie were on their way to a wedding, outfits complete with bouffant hairdos.

Spending time with Grandma Marion and Grandpa Manny in our backyard in Sea Gate. Brooklyn, 1973.

Marion had gone blond years before. That's me, Lisa, on the left and my sister, Robin, on the right.

157

Afterword

"There will come a time here in Brooklyn and all over America, when nothing will be of more interest than authentic reminiscences of the past."

—Walt Whitman

Personal Reminiscences about My Grandmother

GRANDMA MARION AND GRANDPA MANNY LIVED in Brighton Beach, less than two miles from our house in Sea Gate, where I grew up. Even better, Brighton Beach and Sea Gate were connected by the Coney Island boardwalk, so starting about the age of ten, I could ride my bicycle on the boardwalk, on my own, to go visit them.

They lived at 3101 Ocean Parkway, apartment 4J, right off the elevator on the fourth floor. And here is the thing: Marion was such an *amazing* cook, I mean insanely superb, that the delicious smells wafting out of that apartment would make their way into the elevator and down into the main lobby, so that as soon as I pulled open the glass doors of the building entrance, I could smell the mouthwatering *kasha knishes* and pierogen and roasted chicken and sweet-and-sour meatballs that awaited me upstairs. Cooking was no joke to her. Marion was a woman who mulled her own wine from blueberries; owned a professional-grade rotisserie oven, so she could keep crisp chickens rotating on her kitchen counter; and ground her own meat with a contraption that screwed to the countertop because, other than her father and brother, she didn't trust anyone to grind her meat properly. My favorite was her potato soup, with the little floating dumplings.

When I was sick on a school day, to Grandma and Grandpa's apartment I went. Marion would prop me up with pillows on her green velvet couch facing the television, put on *The Price Is Right,* and try to fatten me up with fresh rye bread smothered with butter and scrambled eggs served right in the pan. It was heaven. In third grade, when I was a world-class hypochondriac, I tried to stay home from school every day to go to my grandparents' apartment, concocting all manner of creative symptoms. And for years, my siblings and I went every day to their apartment after school until our parents could pick us up after work. Grandpa Manny would meet us at the Brighton Beach bus stop, immediately take our school bags from us—probably a hundred pounds' worth of books, collectively—and sling them over his shoulder like a sack of flour. My grandparents would break out in song as we entered their apartment.

The apartment itself was physically dark, because it was located in the shadow of the El Train (the elevated New York City subway). But their apartment had a generous, open living area, one bedroom, and a small stand-up kitchen. Every last square inch of the hallway entrance was crammed with credenzas overflowing with my grandfather's books. The carpets were a deep red, and the furnishings ornate and American in style. Heavy wooden chairs with velvet cushions, side tables with carved embellishments, tasseled lamps—all procurements from Mayrock's, the fancy home furnishing store where Marion had worked back in the day. An opulent mirror and fancy crystal bowl full of fake plastic grapes sat atop the bureau that held their *Encyclopædia Britannica,* which my grandfather acquired through years of monthly installment payments. The walls were adorned with Marion's needle-points and with framed collages of black-and-white family photos. For those collages, Marion tended to favor photographs of herself in glamorous poses.

Marion was a total riot. Strong personality, overly dramatic, with a touch of crazy. The kind of woman whom it was tough to have as your mother or mother-in-law, but *awesome* to have as your grandmother. For an example of crazy, as youngsters, anytime we grandchildren were at her place, she insisted on seeing our bowel movements. We were not allowed to flush the toilet before showing her. Never have you heard such expressions of praise and delight over a healthy bowel movement. Totally disgusting, but oh, how I loved it! I felt I'd accomplished something!

Saturday nights, my sisters and I liked to go to my grandparents' apartment for sleepovers. Marion would have us balance pillows on our heads and walk around the living room to observe and compliment us on our posture. Then we would sit on the couch and watch *Dance Fever,* a popular 1980s TV dance competition hosted by Deney Terrio, on which couples tried to win a thousand bucks based on their dance moves. The only problem was that Marion couldn't help getting jealous of us watching the competing couples instead of her, so she would physically stand in front of the television, blocking our view, to demonstrate that she danced better than those contestants. We laughed so hard.

Marion also kept fraying photographs of her old suitors in the apartment. Where, you ask? At the bottom of the napkin basket that sat on the kitchen table. Oh yes, photos of Irving-who-gave-Mama-a-tablecloth and Willie-with-the-bad-hair were there too. She kept them all right there within arm's reach to trot out and show her granddaughters. Whenever she pulled those photos out, as she inevitably did, Grandpa Manny would promptly get up and leave the room to go into his "study" (a bridge table set up in their bedroom). But who's to judge? Marion and Emanuel had one of the most devoted and loving marriages you've ever seen.

Many a Sunday was grandparents' day at our house in Sea Gate. Those Sundays had a rhythm. Marion would stand by the piano and, accompanied by my father, sing a medley of Yiddish songs, including a melodramatic rendition of "My Yiddishe Momme" replete with weeping, before launching into her American favorites, "How Much Is That Doggie in the Window?" and "I Love Paris." Then each of us kids would be required to take turns giving mini-piano recitals. Finally, after eating a meal, we would sit down to play pinochle.

For Marion, a woman who craved both constant attention and activity, it was hard to be the last grandparent and the last of her contemporaries, outliving her husband, her brother, Hymie, and her sister, Ruthie. She was fiercely lonely in her last years, but still fierce.

Let me tell you about one summer evening in 1988, the first time I ever brought a boy home for dinner. I had just graduated from high school, and this boy I was dating was in college. Everyone was home for the summer, including all my siblings, and Grandma Marion was over too. As soon as we sat down to dinner, things started to go downhill. My little brother, Jonathan, a picky eater, immediately refused to eat anything. Then Marion announced she would eat her own food brought from home, and she produced from her purse a half-eaten chicken leg wrapped in crumpled tinfoil. My mom (a terrific cook, really, and a saint) went into the kitchen to warm up Marion's half-eaten chicken leg. Then the fighting broke out between my two older siblings. My older sister, a Columbia undergrad, was in a particularly strident phase and had stopped shaving her armpits to protest the objectification of women. So my older brother, a master provocateur, tried to get a rise out of her by spouting nonsense about how women should be barefoot and pregnant in front of a stove. The yelling that ensued was like the detonation of an incendiary device—my siblings yelling at each other and my parents yelling at them to be quiet. *And then Marion took center stage.* Unwilling to allow others to steal all the attention, at that moment, Grandma Marion dropped her fork on the floor and let out a shriek: "IRA! I CAN'T SEE! I'M BLIND! TAKE ME TO CONEY ISLAND HOSPITAL—I CAN'T SEE!" My date was so overcome that he accidentally spilled an entire glass of water into his lap. No one noticed but me.

In the end, it was Marion's heart that finally gave out. But my grandmother—born Mirka Scheer, who became Marion Scher, who then became Marion Zornberg—did not pass docilely into the next world. Well into her eighties by this point (we think, since her actual birth year remains uncertain), she died like she lived, with vigor. For all her talk of loneliness and wanting to die, once admitted to the hospital with heart failure, she reversed her own prior DNR non-resuscitation instructions and insisted that she be put on life support, trying to make a comeback.

A few days before she passed away, I sat at her bedside in St. Vincent's hospital. She was hooked up to a breathing tube and couldn't talk while I tried to keep her comfortable. Suddenly, her eyes turned animalistic, burning with urgency to tell me something. I tried to guess what was on her mind. *Would you like me to adjust you in the bed?* Vigorous shake of the head. That wasn't it. *You want me to swab your lips with water?* More shaking of the head. Marion was frustrated.

Think, think, *think*, Lisa. What does she want to tell me? A final stab:

The nurses here are worse than Nazis and should rot in hell?

Marion nodded in violent agreement. Yes, that was it! Her body convulsed with relief that I had finally understood. *The nurses are worse than Nazis.* Classic.

Mae West, one of Marion's favorite actresses, famously said, "You only live once, but if you do it right, once is enough." Marion lived a good life. She loved well, she lived fully, and she laid the groundwork for our life here in America. I imagine her now in her version of heaven: at the pinnacle of her youth and glamour in the Catskills, singing, dancing, and laughing, surrounded by her family. Rest in peace, Marion, and thank you for everything.

Acknowledgments

MANY PEOPLE ASSISTED ME ALONG THE journey of researching and writing this book. Thank you to my husband, Matt, first and foremost, for supporting me every inch of the way and sharing in the excitement of each new discovery and fact uncovered.

I thank my wonderful parents. My father, Ira, instilled in me his own love of history and shared insights and family stories with me throughout this process. My mother, Judy, helped gather the photographs for this book, many of which had been damaged in Hurricane Sandy but were preserved through her efforts. (Unfortunately, we were unable to locate any surviving photo of Aunt Annie.) Many thanks too to my siblings for supporting me in this project. Jill shared notes she took years ago of Marion's stories, Robin guided me through publication decisions, and Jonathan spent an awesome evening brainstorming about the proposed movie plots that made their way into Chapter Three. Naomi took me out for airings during the writing process. Many cousins, some whom I already knew and others whom I happily met for the first time through writing this book, shared their memories with me. Thank you.

I am indebted to Barry Moreno, the head librarian of Ellis Island, who was exceptionally generous with his time when I visited him at Ellis Island and bounced, oh, a few hundred questions off him. It was Mr. Moreno who opened my eyes to the pivotal role that HIAS played at Ellis Island in the early 1900s, and who suggested that HIAS might have additional information about the Scheers. He was right.

Shirly Postnikov of HIAS assisted me in searching HIAS's archives and locating records on the Scheers' 1922 odyssey. Ms. Postnikov also sent me, unsolicited, a courtesy copy of *VISAs to Freedom: The History of HIAS,* the outstanding book by Mark Wischnitzer documenting HIAS's work in the first half of the twentieth century. From reading that book, I made the connection that "Attorney Gottlieb," who represented the Scheers during their Washington legal appeals, was none other than Louis Gottlieb, the head of HIAS's Washington bureau.

Many thanks to the descendants of Walter Prendergast, who welcomed my outreach and shared information. It is a joy to know that we are all interconnected, one way or another.

I am grateful to Ancestry.com, Jewish Records Indexing (JRI)-Poland, JewishGen, and YIVO for beautifully archiving and making publicly available all manner of records relating to the Jews of Galicia; and to the US Department of Labor, the US Department of Homeland Security, and the US National Archives, for helping me locate the Scheers' previously unexplored immigration file in the National Archives.

A shout-out to my former colleagues at the US Attorney's Office for the Southern District of New York, with whom I proudly served for sixteen years and who inspired me daily with their relentless commitment to protect America's communities, national security, and the integrity of America's institutions and financial markets. It is not at all surprising that SDNY counts many naturalized citizens and first-generation Americans among its ranks.

Finally, my heartfelt thanks to the professionals who helped make this book look beautiful: Ghislain Viau of Creative Publishing Book Design (cover and interior design), copy editors Daniel Marcus and Joni Wilson, and Alex Salazar of Bob's Photo in Manhasset.

Sources and Notes

Chapter One

On Husiatyn, Kopyczynce, Galicia

Aronson, George. *A Brief History of the Jewish Community in Gusyatin, Ukraine*. Published online by JewishGen KehilaLinks. https://kehilalinks.jewishgen.org/Suchostav/ Gusyatin/Gusyhist.html.

"Galicia," *The YIVO Encyclopedia of Jews in Eastern Europe*. http://www.yivoencyclopedia.org/article.aspx/Galicia.

History of Jewish Communities in Ukraine. http://jewua.org/ husiatyn.

The Last Place in the World—Husiatyn, Ukraine: Lost in Time. https://europebetweeneastandwest. wordpress.com/2016/05/21/ the-last-place-in-the-world-husiatyn-ukraine-lost-in-time.

Polin, Pinkas Hakehillot. *Kopyczynce, Encyclopedia of Jewish Communities in Poland, Volume II*. Published by Yad Vashem (1980) and online on the JewishGen website courtesy of Yad Vashem.

Wrobel, Piotr. "The Jews of Galicia under Austrian-Polish Rule, 1867–1918." *Austrian History Yearbook* vol. 25 (January 1994). Published online by the University of Minnesota Center for Austrian Studies (2009).

Zornberg, Emanuel. *An Account of My Memories, 1914–1925.* (Unpublished. Copy maintained by Lisa Zornberg.)

On Superstition

Jacobs, Joseph and M. Gudemann. "Superstition." *Jewish Encyclopedia* (1906). This contemporaneous article bemoaned the degree to which superstition had woven itself into European Jewish life. The authors decried: "A phenomenon frequent in the history of mankind is repeated here. Stupidity and superstition unite mankind more readily than knowledge and enlightenment."

Also Cited

McCann, Colum. *TransAtlantic.* Random House (2013).

Chapter Two

On American Immigration History and Jews in America

"Irish-Catholic Immigration to America." Library of Congress Website for Teachers. https://www.loc.gov/teachers/classroommaterials/presentationsandactivities/presentations/immigration/alt/irish2.html.

Rogow, Faith. "National Council of Jewish Women." *Jewish Women: A Comprehensive Historical Encyclopedia.* https://jwa.org/encyclopedia/article/National-council-of-jewish-women.

Sachar, Howard M. *A History of Jews in America.* Vintage Books (1992). Chapters I through X, generally.

"The Secret Jewish History of Teddy Roosevelt." *Haaretz* (January 7, 2019). https://www.haaretz.com/us-news/the-secret-jewish-history-of-teddy-roosevelt-1.6811996.

Wischnitzer, Mark. *VISAs to Freedom: The History of HIAS.* Cleveland: The World Publishing Company (1956).

Zornberg, Ira. *Immigration Wars: The History of US Immigration Policies.* (2018).

On Ellis Island, Specifically

"Conditions for Receiving Immigrants at Ellis Island Revolutionized." *Lutheran Woman's Work* vol. 15, no. 6 (June 1922). https://www.gjenvick.com/Immigration/EllisIsland/1922-06-ConditionsForReceivingImmigrantsAtEllisIsland.html.

"Deportation." Cites the spike in deportations in 1922. http://immigrationtounitedstates.org/461-deportation.html.

Ellis Island Foundation. "The Statute of Liberty—Ellis Island." https://www.libertyellisfoundation.org.

Guzda, Henry P. "Keeper of the Gate: Ellis Island a Welcome Site?" *Monthly Labor Review* vol. 109, no. 7 (July 1986), pp. 30–36.

Moreno, Barry. *Children of Ellis Island.* Mt. Pleasant, South Carolina: Arcadia Publishing (2005).

"Reading the Record of Detained Aliens." This is a guide to annotations used by immigration authorities. https://www.jewishgen.org/infofiles/manifests/detained.

Yew, Elizabeth, MD. "Medical Inspection of Immigrants at Ellis Island, 1891–1924." *Bulletin of the New York Academy of Medicine* vol. 56, no. 5 (June 1980).

On the SS *Berengaria*

Hall Genealogy Website. Hosts images of the SS *Berengaria* and reviews its history. https://rmhh.co.uk/ships/pages/berengaria.html. The ship, originally German-owned and

named the *Imperator*, was turned over to England following
the First World War as reparation for the sinking of the
Lusitania. It was then sold to the Cunard Line and became
that company's flagship, renamed the *Berengaria.*

"Passenger Ships Due." *New York Tribune* (September 20, 1922).
Announces anticipated arrival of the SS *Berengaria.*

On the American Eugenics Movement and Harvard's Role

Cohen, Adam S. "Harvard's Eugenics Era." *Harvard Magazine*
(March-April 2016 edition). Calls Harvard the "brain
trust" of the American eugenics movement.

Coolidge, Calvin. "Whose Country Is This?" *Good Housekeeping*
vol. 72, no. 2 (February 1921), pp. 13, 14, 106, 109.

Goldstein, Jared A. "Unfit for the Constitution: Nativism and
the Constitution, from the Founding Fathers to Donald
Trump." *University of Pennsylvania Journal of Constitutional
Law* vol. 20 (2018), pp. 514–515. Discusses formation of
the Immigration Restriction League. https://scholarship.
law.upenn.edu/jcl/vol20/iss3/1.

"Harvard Asks Race and Color of New Students." *New York
Tribune.* (September 20, 1922).

Painter, Nell. "Jim Crow at Harvard: 1923." *New England
Quarterly* vol. 44 (1971).

Sachar, Howard M. *A History of Jews in America.* New York:
Vintage Books (1992). Chapter IX, "Culture Shock and
Eugenics"; Chapter X, "Lawrence Lowell Proposes a Quota."

Singleton, Marilyn M., MD, JD. "The 'Science' of Eugenics:
America's Moral Detour." *Journal of American Physicians
and Surgeons* vol. 19, no. 4 (Winter 2014).

On Jewish American Participation in America's Wars

Sachar, Howard M. *A History of Jews in America.* New York: Vintage Books (1992). Chapter II, "Civil War and Nativization"; Chapter VIII, "The Challenges of Instant Patriotism."

Wolf, Simon. *The American Jew as Patriot, Soldier and Citizen.* New York: The LevyType Company (1895).

"World War II: Statistics on Jewish American Soldiers." Jewish Virtual Library. https://www.jewishvirtuallibrary.org/statistics-on-jewish-american-soldiers-in-world-war-ii.

On the Garment Industry and 1920s Jewish Immigrant Culture

Sachar, Howard. "Jewish Immigrants in the Garment Industry." *My Jewish Learning.* https://www.myjewishlearning.com/article/jewish-garment-workers.

Shepard, Richard F. and Vicki Gold Levi. *Live & Be Well: A Celebration of Yiddish Culture in America.* New York: Ballantine Books (1982).

On Mount Sinai Hospital

The History of The Mount Sinai Hospital. https://www.mountsinai.org/locations/mount-sinai/about/history.

On the Wall Street Bombing of 1920

"Wall Street Bombing 1920." FBI website. www.fbi.gov/history/famous-cases/wall-street-bombing-1920. "Based on bomb attacks over the previous decade, the Bureau initially suspected followers of the Italian Anarchist Luigi Galleani. But the case couldn't be proved, and the anarchist had fled the country. Over the next three years, hot leads turned cold and promising trails turned into dead ends. In the end, the bombers were not identified. The best evidence and analysis since that fateful day of September 16, 1920, suggests that the Bureau's initial thought was correct—that a small group of Italian Anarchists were to blame. But the mystery remains. For the young Bureau, the bombing became one of our earliest terrorism cases—and not the last, unfortunately, to involve the city of New York."

Chapter Three

On the Scheers' Immigration Experience

HIAS Archive. YIVO Archive. Records on HIAS services to the Scheers.

US National Archives. Scheers' Immigration File.

On Simon Wolf

Dalin, David. "Jews and the American Presidency." *Religion, Race, and the American Presidency* (edited by Gaston Espinosa). Lanham, Maryland: Rowman and Littlefield (2018).Chapter 6, pp. 131–132. Calls Simon Wolf the "political confidant of every Republican president from Abraham Lincoln to Taft."

Sachar, Howard M. *A History of Jews in America.* Vintage Books (1992). Chapter III, "Prefigurations of Self-Defense" discusses Wolf's importance in government circles and Wolf's "*qui vive* for Jewish interests before the White House and Congress."

Wolf, Simon. *The American Jew as Patriot, Soldier and Citizen.* New York: The LevyType Company (1895).

Wolf, Simon. *The Presidents I Have Known from 1860 to 1918.* London, UK: Forgotten Press, Classic Reprint (2018). Originally published in 1918 by Byron S. Adams.

On William Musgrave Calder

"Mayor La Guardia at Calder Rites." *New York Times* (March 7, 1945).

"Who's Who in the United States Senate." *The Woman Citizen* (April 1922).

"W. M. Calder Dies, US Ex-Senator, 76." *New York Times* (March 4, 1945).

On Christopher "Christy" Sullivan

"Big Tim for the Senate? It Is Expected that Senator Christy Sullivan Will Make Way for Him." *New York Times* (January 13, 1907).

"The Congress: Christy Sullivan Fades Away." *Time* (December 16, 1940). "In all his years in Congress, Christy had never made a speech."

"Sullivan, Christopher Daniel." Biographical Directory of the United States Congress. http://bioguide.congress.gov/scripts/biodisplay.pl?index=S001051.

On Walter Prendergast

"Brooklyn Investigator Ends 40-Year Career." *New York Times* (October 11, 1964). Announces Walter Prendergast's retirement, describing him as "a chunky bulldog of a man, with steely blue eyes."

"Jacoby Is Appointed Clerk to Surrogate." *New York Times* (May 25, 1943). Announces Walter J. Prendergast's appointment to chief investigator for the Brooklyn District Attorney's Office.

On Nathan Perlman

"Guide to the Nathan Perlman Papers, undated, 1915–1953." Biographical note, American Jewish Historical Society, Center for Jewish History. http://digifindingaids.cjh.org.

Kurt F. Stone. *The Jews of Capitol Hill: A Compendium of Jewish Congressional Members.* Lanham, Maryland: Scarecrow Press, Inc. (2011), pp. 108–110.

"Nathan Perlman, Jurist, 64, Is Dead." *New York Times* (June 30, 1952).

On Albert Rossdale

"Albert B. Rossdale." https://en.wikipedia.org/wiki/.

Kurt F. Stone. *The Jews of Capitol Hill: A Compendium of Jewish Congressional Members.* Lanham, Maryland: Scarecrow Press, Inc. (2011), pp. 93–94.

"Rossdale, Albert Berger." Biographical Directory of the United States Congress. http://bioguide.congress.gov/biosearch/biosearch.asp.

On the US Department of Labor

Ninth Annual Report of the Secretary of Labor for the Fiscal Year Ended June 30, 1921. (Issue date not specified).

Tenth Annual Report of the Secretary of Labor for the Fiscal Year Ended June 30, 1922. (Issued October 1, 1922), quoted at p. 107.

Eleventh Annual Report of the Secretary of Labor for the Fiscal Year Ended June 30, 1923 (October 1, 1923), quoted at p. 45.

On the Emergency Quota Act, the House Floor Debate

Congressional Record, House of Representatives, Wednesday, April 20, 1921. https://www.govinfo.gov/content/pkg/ GPO-CRECB-1921-pt1-v61/pdf/GPO-CRECB-1921- pt1-v61-19-2.pdf.

Representative Cockran remarks quoted at 516–518.

Representative Johnson remarks at pp. 496–501 and quoted at 501.

Representative London remarks quoted at 515.

Representative Parrish remarks quoted at 511.

Representative Rossdale remarks quoted at page 512.

Representative Siegel remarks quoted at 506, 508.

On New York City's Immigration Population

Library of Congress materials: http://www.loc.gov/teachers/ classroommaterials/presentationsandactivities/ presentations/timeline/progress/immigrant/.

The Newest New Yorkers. City of New York (2013). Chapter II, "Growth and Composition of the Immigrant Population."

On Chatham and Phenix National Bank

"The History of Manufacturers Hanover Trust Company." Chase Alumni Foundation. Reviews the history of predecessor banks, including Chatham and Phenix National Bank of New York. https://www.chasealum.org/ article.html?aid=198.

Chapter Four

On Jewish American Response to the Second World War

Sachar, Howard M. *A History of Jews in America.* Vintage Books (1992). Chapter XV, "Mobilization and Jewish Science."

"In contrast with World War I, when large numbers of
Jewish servicemen were immigrant 'Lower East Side boys,'
most Jews of military age in World War II were native-
born."; also discusses how Jewish scientists in America,
many refugee physicists from Nazi Europe, developed the
science behind the atom bomb.

Wischnitzer, Mark. *VISAs to Freedom: The History of HIAS.*
Cleveland: The World Publishing Company (1956).
Chapters Nine and Ten review HIAS's intense efforts
during the Second World War, aiding Jewish refugees to
flee Nazi territory and emigrate elsewhere along whatever
routes remained open; "The mounting anxiety of the Jews
in the United States about their kin in war-torn Europe
found expression in 1941 in 641,655 requests addressed by
HIAS for guidance, counsel, and assistance," p. 173.

Afterword

The Walt Whitman quote is featured by the Green-Wood
Cemetery in Brooklyn.

Made in the USA
San Bernardino, CA
24 April 2019